AUTHOR Heather Newman
DESIGNER AND ILLUSTRATOR Gabriela Schmidt
COPY EDITOR Greg Crawford

———————————————

Published by the Detroit Free Press
600 W. Fort Street
Detroit, MI 48226

ISBN 0-937247-31-6

Dedication

For my parents, Oran and Lynn Brown, who brought home a computer shortly after buying their first microwave. And for my husband, Kevin, who has spent far too many late nights listening to me pound away on our PC.

ACKNOWLEDGEMENTS

This book would not have been possible without the encouragement, ideas and assistance of people around the country.

Thanks go first to all the readers who have written to me with their frustrations and questions over the years; you're the true authors of what appears in my columns. My trusty advisory board of computer experts, whose names you'll see throughout this book, lent a hand.

Next came the able group of editors who put up with my finicky quest for technical accuracy in the columns and all the other trials that come along with working with me: Ron Dzwonkowski, Dale Parry, Sharon Wilmore, Marta Salij and the capable crew on our copy desk.

Special thanks to copy editor Greg Crawford, who had to read nearly everything in this book at least twice, first to get it in the paper and then to get it between these covers. Designer Gabriela Schmidt made this book look great.

And last but not least, had it not been for the suggestion of Free Press Editor Robert McGruder that we collect these columns in one place and the enthusiasm book division chief David Robinson had for pursuing that idea, this volume never would have existed.

I owe you one, fellas.

Heather

FROM THE ILLUSTRATOR: To my mom, dad and sister, my beautiful family & friends, con todo mi amor de Gabi.

Contents

PC@HOME

Getting started

Welcome!

More than two years ago, the Free Press started publishing a Sunday page of computer advice called pc@home. I had been working at the paper for a little less than a year and was coming off a stint as author of a weekly computer column that ran in newspapers across this country and abroad. Fortunately for me, Free Press features editor Dale Parry thought the new page and my column were a good match, and they debuted in Detroit together.

What you're holding is a compilation of the best material we've published since then. It has been edited and updated, and we hope it gives you a boost in making the most of your PC.

The book covers the basics of computers and the Internet in plain English. I also look at new products, services and software and tell you whether they live up to their hype.

Studies show that the majority of you have access to computers at work and at home. Half of you have access to the Internet in one of those places. But chances are that the nerd box could be doing more for you than it is now. That's where this book comes in. It can show you how to get the most out of your microchips.

For instance, does your strawberry jam refuse to jell? Does your Saturn refuse to start? You can get culinary, automotive and other advice from 30 million friends on the Internet by using just e-mail and your wits. We'll talk about how to reach folks through discussion group "lists."

Can't get your computer to acknowledge the new hard drive that you so painstakingly screwed in, connected and powered up? It could be just a matter of moving a tiny plastic piece on the back called a jumper. Learn about it when we talk about adding a second drive.

See a picture on the Internet that you want to use as the background on your computer screen? With Netscape and Windows, just use the button on the right side of your mouse on the picture and choose Set as Wallpaper.

There are other Netscape tips in the Internet section.

Over the next few chapters, we'll also do Windows, explain the meaning of those computer acronyms people are forever throwing around — from OS to IRQ to RAM — and steer you to some nifty Web sites that help you keep a handle on everything from your bottom line to your waistline.

The focus here is always practical, easy and quick. My goal is to give you the tools you need to make your machine work for you, instead of the other way around.

If you like the book, you can do me a favor.

I've been using personal computers for 19 years and have been on-line for 17. I've used nearly every major program on the market and have become comfortable with both IBM-compatible and Apple machines. I've gotten pretty good at troubleshooting hardware and software problems and have developed a nose for good stuff on-screen and on-line.

But experience isn't everything. My column won't continue to be helpful unless I know what you need. So here's my first and only request of you, computer users or wanna-bes: Contact!

By snail mail, e-mail or fax, tell me what kind of computer you're using and how you like it. What kinds of software do you use? Do you use a straight Internet service provider, America Online or CompuServe? What do you want to do with computers that you aren't doing now?

And a special request for the advanced folks out there: Do you live, breathe and eat computers? Do you troubleshoot software or hardware for a living and set up networks in your sleep? I've chosen a select group of techies to be on the advisory board for my column. They answer a question every month or two from me by phone or by e-mail. In exchange, they see their names in my columns and have the satisfaction of knowing they have helped out computer owners everywhere. Want to join? Just e-mail me with your qualifications.

In either case, enjoy. It's been a fun two years. I'm looking forward to many more.

Heather Newman
Detroit Free Press
600 W. Fort Street
Detroit, MI 48226
Fax: 313-223-4436
e-mail: newman@freepress.com
See my most recent columns on-line at **www.freep.com/tech /pcathome** . ∎

Having fun with your PC

Maybe that computer you got for the holidays is still sitting in the box and waiting for you to turn it on.

Or maybe you're a computer expert, and using the machine has gotten dull.

Either way, it's time for a resolution: This is the year you have fun with your PC.

A great idea, you say, but you've been resolving to lose that last 10 pounds for 10 years, and that hasn't happened either. Never fear! Follow some of these suggestions and you might actually look forward to hitting the "on" button:

NARROW YOUR FOCUS. One reason we get frustrated when learning how to use computers is because we want to do everything at once. We don't expect college students to learn all their subjects at once, but we expect ourselves to absorb checkbook balancing, newsletter publishing, Web surfing, e-mail writing and game playing all at once on our PCs.

Give yourself a break and pick one program you're going to get really good at this year. Learn that one well enough, and I guarantee you'll be able to transfer some of that knowledge to other programs. You'll at least have the warm glow of knowing that you're an expert at one thing.

If you're going to wander the World Wide Web this year, do the same thing: Pick one subject area and become an expert on those Web sites. Learn to bookmark the sites you like, and keep a list of the places you've been. Pick something fun: Learning everything there is to know about stained glass on the Web is a lot more fun than sifting through tax law. (Unless you REALLY love tax law, in which case, go for it.)

MAKE FRIENDS. There's nothing better than finding information about a topic you like on-line — unless it's talking to other people who are interested in that topic. By using forums that have been set up on Web sites or e-mail discussion groups (also known as lists), you can read other people's conversations about your area of interest — or join in. To learn more about joining a list, go to the Internet

section of this book.

PLAY A GAME. Don't skip over the game aisle when you head into your favorite software store. There's an incredible variety of computer games out there, and they're not all shoot-'em-ups. Adventure games like Riven or Grim Fandango can take you through beautiful worlds, and you'll solve puzzles as you go. Strategy games like StarCraft and Command and Conquer let you plan campaigns. Flight simulators show you the skies. Virtually every puzzle you can buy in real life has an excellent computer form.

TEACH YOUR OLD PC NEW TRICKS. If software seems a bit expensive (new games can cost $50-$80), try the wonderful world of shareware and freeware programs.

With freeware, you never have to pay; with shareware, you're asked to send in a modest donation to cover the programmer's costs.

This is a great way to get new games or even those practical programs you'd like to have without paying a mint. Two good places to look: CNET's **www.download.com** and ZDNet's **www.hotfiles.com** .

GET ON-LINE. I know, you've heard a lot of bad things about pornographers, junk mail senders and pedophiles on the Internet. But it also has the largest and fastest-growing collection of documents available. And it's the biggest local calling area in the world when you consider that you can talk to people in Israel or Brazil without running up a long-distance charge.

To get started, you'll need a modem — most new computers come with them — and an Internet account. America Online, which, it seems, has offered 100 free on-line hours to everyone on the planet, is one way to connect to the Net. And it offers some nice, restrictive controls for your children's e-mail accounts, if you don't want them getting mail from strangers.

But your local Internet service providers, or ISPs, can get you hooked up as well. Check in the yellow pages under "Internet."

And start having some fun! ▪

Sit right to avoid pain

Some folks spend so much time at the computer, it hurts.

I don't mean they become geeks without social lives. I mean that ordinary people, using computers at work and at home, can put themselves in such awkward positions for so many hours that their bodies start to rebel.

Their necks, shoulders, wrists and backs start to complain. Finally, it becomes less painful just to skip computing altogether. But by arranging a few things in your work area and by keeping a few simple tips in mind, you can reduce the pain.

These tips may be especially important for children if they've started surfing the Net or playing games for hours at a time. Their bodies may repair themselves faster, but they can still injure themselves over time.

START WITH THE CHAIR. It should be low enough to allow you to put both feet flat on the ground comfortably without any pressure on the back of your thighs. If you can't, try putting phone books or other props where your feet usually rest.

Your posture should be upright with an imaginary straight line connecting the top of your head to your tailbone on the chair. Leaning forward or back can tire your back and shoulder muscles. If your chair doesn't allow you to sit that way, you may want to consider dragging one in from the dining room or an office conference room; the fixed backs often help you sit upright.

CONSIDER WHERE YOUR MONITOR IS POSITIONED. Many people put their screen on top of their computer. But for most folks, that raises it too high. For the least strain on your neck, you should be looking straight ahead or even slightly down at the screen.

Wrists are especially sensitive to repetitive computing injuries, and there's a good reason: While you're typing or mousing, they're always moving. Ideally, you want a low desk or a computer keyboard tray to place the keyboard about level with your waist. You want your wrists to be relaxed and horizontal while your fingers are touching the keys.

If your desk is too high but a keyboard tray would be too low, you can try using a taller chair (with something to prop your feet on) to raise your arms to the right level. Be sure your mouse is on the same level as your keyboard.

If you're having wrist pain, you might consider trying to switch to a trackball or ergonomic mouse that lets you hold your wrist in a more natural position. One product actually allows you to hold the mouse like a joystick, hitting the so-called fire button on the top to click. Another lets you point a light pen at the screen, skipping the mouse altogether.

TAKE FREQUENT BREAKS. Get up every 15 minutes or so and stretch. Both your eyes and your muscles will thank you.

FINALLY, LEARN THE KEYBOARD SHORTCUTS IN YOUR MOST FREQUENTLY USED PROGRAMS. Part of the strain in computing comes from switching constantly from keyboard to mouse and back again. If you can use the keyboard to perform common commands without having to use the mouse to pick those commands out of menus, you can avoid a bit of repetitive movement.

Most programs have the keyboard shortcuts in their manuals, but you can often find them in the menus themselves. Look carefully the next time you pull down a command; written next to it in the menu may be the keyboard shortcut to make that command happen, such as Ctrl-C for copy or Ctrl-V for paste. Some commands, like those two, are often the same in many programs.

Good luck, and take these suggestions seriously. Even if you've been computing for years, pain can strike when you least expect it. ■

TAKE FREQUENT BREAKS.

Get up every 15 minutes or so and stretch. Both your eyes and your muscles will thank you.

Hardware

Buying a
computer

The jargon

Call this a geek speak primer.

A lot of readers have written and called about specific computer troubles, topics they'd like to see covered here and experiences they've had with your PCs. One thing I've heard over and over again is your frustration with some help desk personnel who rattle off computer jargon so quickly you feel they need a secret decoder ring.

You may be familiar with some of these basic terms from buying your PC. You may have learned and forgotten others. Here's a refresher:

CPU: Central Processing Unit, or the box where your computer's guts are stored.

PROCESSOR: The fancy computer chip that acts as the brains of your machine. Techs will refer to your machine by what kind of a chip is inside. For example, they might call your PC a Pentium III 500. That means that it has an Intel Pentium III chip inside that's running the show at 500 megahertz. Processors designed for mobile computing are slower than desktop models, even though the model and clock speed, or "hertz" number, may sound the same.

PENTIUM MMX, PENTIUM II, PENTIUM III: Intel processors. The Pentium III is faster than the Pentium II, which is faster than the Pentium MMX, even at the same clock speed.

RAM: Your computer's short-term memory. The PC uses it to hold whatever it's working on at a particular point in time, then erases it. Think of it this way: When you look up a phone number, then repeat it over and over again in your head until you dial, then promptly forget it, you've just used your human version of RAM.

HARD DISK: Where your computer stores its long-term memory. Anything you (or your computer) saves to the hard disk, or hard drive, is stored there until someone makes the decision to erase it later. If you have your mother's phone number memorized and can call it up in your head at will, it's stored in your human version of a hard disk.

CACHE: Additional memory that holds instructions created by programs using RAM that are waiting for the processor to perform them.

MEGABYTE: 1 million bytes, or enough space to store about 200,000 words of text.

GIGABYTE: 1 billion bytes.

MOTHERBOARD: A big piece of plastic that links together all your computer's innards. Your processor, RAM and hard disk are all plugged into this board, either directly or with cables.

CARD AND SLOT: Many add-ons to your PC come in the form of cards. They are literally plastic pieces with electronic components attached to them that plug into the motherboard. The ridges on the motherboard that cards plug into are called slots.

IRQ: Short for "interrupt request." These are like CB channels that your computer uses to communicate with its separate parts. If two parts of your computer — such as your modem and your mouse — are using the same IRQ, the computer gets confused and neither one works. This afflicts only PCs, not Apples or their clones.

OPERATING SYSTEM OR OS: A software program that tells your computer's hardware what to do. Windows is an operating system; so is MacOS.

AUTOEXEC.BAT, CONFIG.SYS OR ANY FILE THAT ENDS IN .INI: These are files that PCs (not Apples or their clones) use to figure out how to run. Every time you turn on a PC, it does everything that autoexec.bat and config.sys tell it to. When you run a program, it checks its initializing file, which ends in .ini, to see what settings to use.

THE REGISTRY: This is a file in Windows 95 and 98 that contains detailed system settings for every part of your PC, both hardware and software. Editing the Registry is recommended only for the most advanced users.

CD-ROM: The drive in your

computer that plays CDs.

CD-R: A CD-ROM drive that can write on CDs once. These are much slower at reading CD-ROMs than a normal drive, but they can create CDs of your own.

CD-RW: A CD-R drive that can write on discs more than once. Also a slow reader for the most part. Many people choose a CD-R or CD-RW drive as a second drive, rather than a CD-ROM replacement.

DVD OR DVD-ROM: These play high-density CD-like discs. They're slower for things like games, but can display movies on your computer screen. A DVD-ROM drive often replaces the CD-ROM.

PASSIVE VS. ACTIVE COLOR: Passive screens on laptop or notebook computers are not as good or as active in very bright or very dark conditions or when viewed from an angle. Active color screens are also known as active matrix or TFT (thin film transistor) screens.

CONTRAST RATIO: Measures how crisp the screen contrast looks. Often used for evaluating laptop computers.

VIDEO RAM, SGRAM: Video memory used to draw pictures on the screen. (SGRAM means screen graphics RAM.) This may also be found in a description of a computer's graphics card, where it may be identified solely as RAM or SDRAM.

50X (OR 44X, OR 40X) CD-ROM: CD-ROM drive that transmits data 50 (or 44, or 40) times faster than the first CD-ROMs built.

NETWORK OR ETHERNET CARD: A piece of plastic inside the PC that lets it communicate using cables with other PCs in your home.

MODEM: A card inside your PC that lets you communicate with other PCs using your phone lines.

MONITOR: Your desktop computer's screen.

USB PORTS: Small, square plugs that are used by accessories such as scanners or cameras. Theoretically, they don't require the user to install any software to run the device, and they can detect when a device has been plugged in and what it is. In reality, that doesn't work all the time, but reliability is coming.

PARALLEL PORT: The rectangular plug in the back of your PC where the printer typically is attached. This is frequently used for external accessories like scanners or Zip drives. ■

Processors: Your computer's brain

Walk into a computer store these days and you'll have more to consider than Compaq, Dell or Hewlett-Packard. You're also going to have to choose among Intel, AMD and Cyrix; Pentium III, K6-III and MII; or Celeron, Athlon and WinChip2.

There are a dozen processor chips, each working as the brains of your computer, to choose from. All this just when you thought the computer alphabet soup couldn't get any worse.

The good news is that this confusing mess is the result of new competition between other chip companies and market giant Intel, which means better computer prices for you. The bad news is that you now have to track brand names to be sure you're buying what you want.

I'll give you a cheat sheet, but first, the answer to your other question:

Why didn't they just keep naming these things 386, 486, 586, etc., as they did with older computers? No matter who made the chip, it was still a 386, and that made it easy to shop.

In Intel's opinion, it was a little TOO easy to shop. The company couldn't trademark a number, so its competitors cheerfully named their chips after Intel's. That made it hard to figure out whether you were buying from the world's biggest processor maker or one of the new kids.

So starting with the 586, Intel switched to names such as Pentium that it could trademark.

Two things you need to know: First, chips are identified by a model name (like K6-III or Pentium III) and a clock speed, measured in megahertz (Mhz). The clock speed identifies how quickly the processor can handle new instructions. In general, the larger the number, the faster the chip.

Second, chips are also identified by how much level 2 cache (pronounce it "cash") they have. The level 2 cache is additional memory that holds the instructions before the processor gets them. The more cache you have, the better.

All the speed comparisons here are from PC Magazine's labs, which periodically test the chips.

Intel controls the majority of the processor market, with most of its dominance in higher-end PCs. (AMD starts to take over in the lower end.) Its best-performing chips are from the Pentium II and III line, and they can hold their own with virtually every processor on the market. If you've got the money (and you don't want to buy an Apple computer, many of which today run on Apple-only G4 chips), you can't go wrong with a Pentium III.

Pentium MMX PCs, the precursor to the Pentium II, are still in some stores. But they've been replaced by a new name: the Celeron. Many Celerons have less cache than a Pentium II, and so run more slowly than the Pentium II, the

AMD K6-2 or the Cyrix MII. Celerons faster than 300 Mhz have the same amount of cache as the Pentium II, run as quickly and, if you can still find them, are often cheaper. (If it's exactly 300 Mhz, look for the "a" after the speed to make sure it's a Celeron with a level 2 cache.)

Most new computers will have either the Pentium II or Pentium III inside.

AMD has its K6-2 and K6-III, including 3DNow! instructions, which help its chip handle complex floating-point calculations more quickly. You won't see the effect of those instructions except in 3D games that have been written specifically to take advantage of them. (Check the box for your games to see whether they were.) If the game isn't written for 3DNow!, it'll run faster on a Pentium II or III at the same clock speed than on an equivalent K6-2 or K6-III. If it has been, it'll run a little faster on the AMD K6-2 or K6-III.

Business programs, and just about everything other than 3DNow!-enabled games, run about the same on equivalent K6-2 and Pentium II chips. K6-III chips are a bit faster than Pentium III chips at the same clock speed.

Cyrix, a subsidiary of National Semiconductor, produces the MII. That chip runs about 10 percent to 15 percent slower than the K6-2 or the Pentium II; a version is available with the 3DNow! instruction set.

IDT is a new name in the market, but you'll see a lot more of it; the company just signed a foundry agreement with IBM, which will let it make more chips. Its WinChip2 runs as fast as Pentium II chips with the same clock speed. It also produces a slower WinChip C6, which you'll see mostly in PCs costing less than $500. Look for the letters "3D" after its chip names if you want to be sure you have the 3DNow! instruction set. ∎

Prices are getting even nicer

Your next PC may be as cheap as a nice TV.

Ever since Microworkz in Seattle announced in mid-1999 that it would begin selling respectably equipped Cyrix MII 300-based computers for $299, including a year of Internet access and the Corel suite of business software, other makers have been dropping prices.

The rock-bottom prices are part of a happy trend for PC users who don't want or need the latest power and features. Everyone wants Aunt Erma to buy a PC, and that's leading to terrific buys.

Internet providers everywhere have begun giving away PCs if you sign up for two years of Internet service (at a rate that's only $5-$10 a month more than what some national providers are charging). If these deals succeed, expect to see this pricing pop up everywhere as people start to think of PCs like cell phones: something to give away to lock you into a service contract.

And then there are the I-don't-care-about-privacy, just-get-me-on-line shoppers. Free-PC made big news this year when it offered free PCs and Internet access to select people who were willing to fill out intensive questionnaires about their habits and lives, which were then shared with advertisers, who then got to fill the people's screens with ads tailored to their tastes.

NetZero is following this model for Internet access. (See **www.netzero.com** or **www.free-pc.com** for details on these deals. If you're not on-line at home, you can usually find a public access terminal at your local library.) With NetZero, your e-mail and Web access are free, but you have to fill out a questionnaire about your habits and put up with constant ads.

Whether these services succeed depends on the rates advertisers are willing to pay and how many people they view as desirable choose to sign up. Phone companies in Great Britain are offering free Internet access as a way to woo customers. We've seen a little of that here in the States, as long-distance providers slash rates on Net service for customers to keep their phone business (Think AT&T WorldNet and MCI WorldCom, for example.) You'll see a lot more deals like these. ■

Basic questions when buying a PC

Computers are at the top of a lot of folks' gift lists, and no wonder. They're faster, cheaper and easier than ever before. Must-have accessories have finally dropped to reasonable prices, and there are numerous good brands to choose from.

In buying a computer for your home, the first thing you should know is that virtually every name-brand computer is made with the same types of parts. Just a few companies dominate the hard drive market, for example, so most computer makers buy from the same two or three suppliers. Often, the internal CD-ROM drive is made by the people from whom you would buy one if you were adding to a machine later.

Before you decide which machine you want to buy, you have some decisions to make.

INTEL-COMPATIBLE PC OR APPLE MACINTOSH?
Zealots on both sides will bury you with information about these competing systems. There are tradeoffs regardless of which machine you choose.

Most personal computers in stores have an Intel-compatible processor chip for a brain. They run some kind of Windows as their basic operating system. Lots of software is available for Windows machines, but the processor chips they use are slower than new ones for Apples.

Apple computers run off a different kind of chip and have their own operating system, MacOS. Though you can run Windows programs on Apple computers by using add-on software or hardware, that setup is slower and more problematic than running those programs in Windows.

Much less software is available for MacOS than for Windows. You will be able to find examples of nearly every type of software for the Mac, but you might not find the specific program you want.

So shop for software first by browsing store or on-line catalogs (such as **www.zones.com**). If the software you want to use is available for MacOS, give the Apple computers some serious consideration. For example, iMacs are fast, though hard to upgrade. They make good first computers.

If you don't find the software you want or you must be fully compatible with PCs at work, buy a PC.

WHICH BRAND?
Consider four things: warranty, longevity, price and convenience, in that order of importance.

Look for a warranty of at least a year, preferably two or three. Find out up front where you have to take the computer if it breaks — PC parts aren't infallible. Best is on-site service, offered by many top manufacturers for the first year. It means the company's technicians will come to you and fix the machine free of charge. Next best is the option to drop it off at nearby store. Worst is to have to ship the PC to another state.

Before you buy an extended warranty offered by a store, scrutinize its terms. They often offer little more than the manufacturer gives you.

Next, consider how long the company has been in business and its chances of staying in business for the life of your machine. A great warranty means nothing if the company has shut down and left no forwarding address.

If the company hasn't been in business long, research the firm at your library and on the Internet. Any financial weakness can be a bad sign. Three places to start: Free Press articles at **www.freep.com**, CNet computer news service at **www.news.com** and Ziff-Davis, computer magazine publisher, at **www.zdnet.com** .

If the warranty is good and the company is solid, move on to price. If you're getting the same innards backed by the same warranty, there are few cases in which it's wrong to buy the cheaper machine.

STORE OR MAIL ORDER?
The best prices on computers are often found in catalogs and on-line, not on store shelves. You can often specify

exactly what hardware and software you want to have installed on your new machine.

However, ordering a computer over the phone or over the Web usually means you're the one who has to plug in all the wires when it arrives. It also means you can't try out the machine until you've bought it.

Always be extra careful when ordering by mail to make sure you can return the computer to a local dealer. You don't want to have to ship it to Alaska to get it fixed.

"While brand may or may not be important in everyone's eyes, you still have to ask the question, 'Who will fix it when it breaks?' " said Bill Bajcz, president of Megatechnologies, Inc. in Milford, Mich. "And it will, sooner or later."

Technical support is also important. Is the call for help toll-free? Is the line active 24 hours a day, seven days a week?

"Some mail-order houses give a Japanese warranty, and that and a quarter won't get you a computer fixed in the United States," said Marcie V. Smith, owner of One Stop Internet in Oak Park, Mich.

If you decide to buy from a store, it's best to pick one that specializes in computers.

Warning signs to look for: stores that sell only one brand of computer; salespeople who also cover other departments, like small appliances; an extremely limited selection and a restrictive return or service policy.

You don't want to have to mail your computer back to the manufacturer if you bought it next door; that's why you shopped in a store in the first place.

WHICH PROCESSOR CHIP? See the article a few pages before this one on the different processors. You

should have one in mind when you walk into the store or surf the Web.

WHAT SPECS? To figure out exactly what you want in your new machine, use this method: Go into the computer store and head for the software, not the machines. Browse for programs you might like to run, particularly the ones that demand the most from your computer: 3D design programs for your house, 3D games, databases for your small business.

Don't let salespeople bother you yet. You're still doing your basic research.

"When a buyer walks into a big store with bright lights, it is easy to get caught up in the latest fads and gadgets," said Ronald Draayer, head of the computer department at Davenport College in Grand Rapids, Mich. "You need to decide ahead of time what your priorities are, without any salesperson trying to sell you the latest toy that you know nothing about."

Note what each program you're considering requires to run. You'll find that in the specifications on the side of the box. This is the minimum level of hardware you must have; most software will run better if you buy a bit more than what's required.

If you can afford it, you should always try to buy more than the minimum. The software you've chosen will run faster, and you'll be less likely to need an upgrade six months from now

when the new version of that software arrives and has features you can't live without.

Sumir Meghani, a recent West Bloomfield (Mich.) High School graduate and World Wide Web page developer, pointed out that even simple programs can take more resources if you want to run them all at the same time.

"As a student, sometimes I have a CD-ROM encyclopedia, Netscape, Microsoft Word and a chat program open at the same time," he said.

The further above the minimum requirements you buy, the longer you'll be able to go before you need an upgrade or a new PC.

"It always comes down to two things," said Sandy Kronenberg, chief executive of Defrag Inc., a Farmington Hills, Mich., computer communications company. "What's your budget, and how long do you want it to last?"

If you think you might want to keep your computer longer and upgrade (as opposed to buying a new

machine later), be sure to look for things that make upgrading easier: extra bays on the front of the machine for new drives and extra slots inside for cards used by modems, scanners and the like.

If you can, speak with a salesperson in the store or on the phone and determine how many of the computer's basic parts are proprietary — that is, parts that require you to buy the same brand if you upgrade later. Sometimes proprietary parts mean that upgrades are impossible — the computer can't handle better or faster models of its components. Other times, you're stuck buying just that one brand of part, no matter what the cost or how powerful it is.

Finally, be sure to pack as much into your PC as you can afford. Think of it like buying a car: Accessories are a lot cheaper if you negotiate for them up front than if you add them later, says Mike Bader of LAN Solutions in Ferndale, Mich.

What you're likely to find on that list of minimum specs:

THE PROCESSOR: Most software now requires a Pentium II chip or the equivalent speed in other brands.

THE RAM: Always buy more than your minimum; it's relatively cheap and makes the biggest difference in increasing the speed of your programs. Also called SDRAM.

SGRAM: If you're going to be running games or intense graphics programs, make sure you have at least 8-16 megabytes of video memory.

THE HARD DRIVE SPACE: More is better. Sure, you may not be creating and editing movies on your PC. But those programs you want to buy are getting bigger every year. Office

2000, for example, takes 525 megabytes of space for its Premium version. That's a chunk.

THE CD-ROM DRIVE: Playing movies requires a DVD-ROM, or digital versatile disc, drive. Other programs run on compact discs, which can be used with regular CD-ROM or DVD-ROM drives. CD-ROM drives are faster than DVD-ROMs, so they tend to be better for high-end 3D games and other intensive disc users. (Shoot for high "x" numbers for those drives.)

CD-R AND CD-RW: These are recordable compact disc drives. CD-R drives allow you to record on a CD once. CD-RW drives use more expensive discs and allow you to record multiple times on the same disc. (They can also record once on plain CD-R discs.) They're useful for backup, creating custom music mixes or transporting large files.

THE MODEM: Accept nothing less than 56 kilobits per second and make sure that the listing says it's "v.90 compatible." That's the language that most modems use to talk to one another.

THE MONITOR: There's one thing to decide that won't be determined by your software's minimum requirements: your monitor. Common sizes range from 14 inches to 19 inches, measured diagonally. Large models are much more expensive than small ones.

Look for a tiny dot pitch (the size of the dots that make up the picture on the screen): 0.28 is OK; 0.25 is better. And be sure you look at the monitor when it's on: Some don't display pictures to the edge of the screen, meaning you may end up paying

more for less viewing area. There also are notable differences in how the screens look, much like different TVs show different pictures.

Many advertised prices for computer systems omit the monitor; be careful when comparing prices.

Other items you'll see in the specs at the computer store:

NETWORK CARD: Unless you have two PCs at home you want to hook together with a cable, you don't need one. See the section on hooking two computers together later in this section.

OPERATING SYSTEM: Computers usually ship with Windows 98 or Windows NT. NT is an office or advanced version of 98, and it is a little more stable. But it is occasionally incompatible with programs that run in 98.

If you choose NT, be sure to double-check every piece of software you buy from now on to make sure it will run with NT.

SLOTS/BAYS: These let you add things to your computer later, so you want as many free slots and bays as possible. There are two kinds of slots inside a PC: ISA, the long ones, and PCI, the short ones. You want plenty of both. Bays are the spaces in the front of the machine where you put drives, like your CD-ROM, magnetic cartridge drive or CD writer.

Find out how much you can expand your RAM (and whether there are any open RAM slots, which are shorter still), how many empty card slots you have and how many empty bays you have. A good bet would be six open slots, two open bays and two open RAM slots. But it won't kill you to take less. ■

Should you upgrade or buy new?

Whenever someone starts handing out advice on what new computer to buy, most of us with older machines are left with a burning question: Is it time to get rid of our PCs and buy new — or should we just fix them up?

Work through this eight-step process to find out whether it's time for you to spend more money, and how.

1. Does your computer work?

Nothing can make a new computer purchase more appealing than a sudden betrayal by your old machine. If your computer works, move to step 2. If not, skip to step 4.

2. Can you run everything that you consider vital?

What's vital is going to depend on you. If your machine can't handle that small business software that you think is essential to running your home office, then you're likely to need a serious upgrade or a new PC. On the other hand, if you can do everything you need, but can't run that newest 3D shoot-'em-up . . . well, you might want to wait. If you can't run what you can't live without, move to step 4. Otherwise, move on to step 3.

3. Can you run everything you want?

If so, move to step 8b. If you can't but you're determined to get that new program running, go to step 4.

4. Is it an easy upgrade or fix? Can you do it yourself? Or are you willing to learn how to fix it?

If all you need to run the latest program is a quick injection of RAM, it's a simple two-step upgrade: Pop the box and add more cards. (And jump down to step 8b.)

On the other hand, replacing your old hard drive with a new one and moving your files from one to the other can be a real headache. Is this repair worth the time and hassle it will take? Even if it means hours with manuals and on hold with tech support? Good for you; fix your machine and jump to 8b.

If you're not the fix-it type, go to step 5.

5. Are you willing to pay someone to upgrade or fix your machine?

My rule of thumb: If you're going to spend more than about $200 on a repair, don't do it. New, baseline PCs run $500 and are almost guaranteed to be faster than your old machine. You can even reuse your monitor, printer and accessories to save some extra cash on the purchase. Are your repairs going to cost less than $200? Do the work; go to step 8b. Are they going to cost more than $400? Go to step 6.

If they're in between, are you will-ing to pay that much to keep your old PC running? If yes, pay the repair bill and move to step 8b. If not, go to step 6.

6. Can you pay cash for a new machine?

If not, go to step 8b. Computers are about the worst thing you can buy on credit because they're not worth anything by the time you pay them off. Leases are even worse than putting your computer on a credit card.

Until you save up, you can always visit your local library to use its computers. (You can get access to e-mail by using free Web-based e-mail services, such as HotMail at **www.hotmail.com**). If you can afford to pay cash now, move to step 7.

7. Do you need it right now?

Keep this rule of thumb in mind: For every month that you wait, the price of your selected computer system will probably drop about $100. That's no joke. At some point, you're going to have to quit reading the ads and leap. But if you can wait a month or two, move to 8b. If not, go to 8a.

8a. Go for it!

You're ready, willing and able to buy a new PC, and it should be a good household tool. Be prepared: In about two years, you're going to want to take this quiz again. It's hard to keep up when the industry moves this fast.

8b. Wait!

It's not the right time for you to buy a new PC. Wait a month. Take this quiz again and see whether the results change . . . and congratulate yourself on your restraint. ■

Apple vs. IBM-compatible PC

Apple computers or Intel-chip PCs? MacOS or Windows?

This isn't just a computer shopping question. It's a religious quest.

Geeks who grew up with amber-on-black screens of DOS commands look on Apple computers with suspicion. Their friendly, smiling icons, their chirpy chimes — why, no real computer could be so lighthearted.

Apple users, on the other hand, consider many PC owners to be idiots.

Those PC types have bought years of "Wintel" public relations, helping Windows (Microsoft) and PC chip maker Intel take over the world, they say. And, of course, there's the old joke: What was the first name for Windows 95? MacOS 84. And so, every time I write even a paragraph about Macintoshes, I get a pile of mail from PC owners wondering why we're giving even the tidbit of space we do to Macs and from Mac owners ready to torch my desk for not devoting the ENTIRE column to Apples — or for saying something they consider uncomplimentary.

Take one recent article on how to buy a PC. I mentioned two Mac models and noted Apple's (then) declining market share. As usual, it touched off a torrent of virulent e-mail.

Let me just say about the dozens of Apple users who wrote to tell me that Macintoshes ROSE in the market in the beginning of 1998. What they all neglected to mention was that the rise — from 3.75 percent to 4 percent of the total PC market — barely canceled out the losses Apple suffered in 1997. (It had 4 percent market share at the end of the first quarter 1997, too.)

And let's note that Apple had 10 percent of the market five years ago.

Finally, one more bit of news: Ziff-Davis, publisher of a pile of computing magazines, released a 1998 U.S. customer loyalty poll, measuring how often 11,440 people who buy a particular brand of computer buy it again.

Apple had led that poll in previous years. In 1998, Apple dropped to third, behind Gateway and Hewlett-Packard. Its repurchase rate dropped 11 percent to 71 percent (compared with Gateway, which had 75 percent). Among nonbusiness customers, it dropped 30 percent.

Why is that important if you want to buy a Mac? With fewer people using Macs, more software makers may decide it isn't worth the expense to make a second version of their software that will run on Apple machines.

For now, Mac owners argue, there are plenty of applications out there. And that's true: You'll find at least one version of nearly every type of software to run on the Mac. But you might not find a copy of your favorite program, and whether the number will increase depends on Apple's fluctuating market share.

That isn't to say that Apples can't come back. They're wonderfully friendly to use. The G4 is a powerful machine, and the iMac appeals to basic home users. Apple will continue to dominate the resource-intensive graphics, photo and layout industry. There's a reason why the Detroit Free Press and most other North American newspapers are designed and laid out using Macintoshes.

The only way that niche will fade is if Adobe and other graphics software makers stop supporting Macs. It hasn't happened. But if the Apple market shrinks again?

The sky isn't falling for Apples. But I don't usually recommend them to people who buy new PCs because of the limited selection of software (and the generally higher prices). Why pay the same price or more for a machine that won't run as much?

Yes, I know. Apple owners everywhere are opening up their e-mail programs to tell me. Why? Because it's a better machine!

But is it? Really?

What's starting to give me a chuckle is how similar Macs and PCs have become. Windows 95 lifted some of MacOS's best qualities. New versions of MacOS have, in turn, stolen features from Windows 98 and NT.

Moving from a Mac to a PC and back again used to require major mental adjustment. But they're both starting to look a lot alike on the screen. For a casual user, is there really a difference?

I say no. And that, I guarantee you, will have BOTH dedicated PC techies and Mac addicts filling my mailbox.

See how much you have in common?

(**NOTE:** A few months after this column ran, Apple released the iMac, which has been a resounding success — compared with standard Apple models, at least. The iBook notebook also promises to catch consumers' eyes. Although the software selection for MacOS continues to be fairly dismal, I'm pleased to say that the company has slowly been growing in market share. If you're happy with the programs that are available for MacOS without using Windows-simulation hardware or software, there's no reason not to buy an Apple; the company's future, while not assured, looks brighter than it has in years.)

Buying accessories

Quick quiz: What part of your computer will you use the longest?

Chances are, your printer. Long after the main box, the monitor, the mouse and all the rest have hit the trash heap, you might still be watching that same old printer churn out your master-pieces.

So consider carefully what you buy. Printers come in two flavors: ink jet and laser jet. Ink-jet printers spray a fine mist of ink on the page, while lasers use toner and heat like a regular copy machine.

There are advantages and disadvantages to both. Ink jets are cheaper, especially if you want color. Their cartridges are also cheaper. But they tend to be slower (because rushing the job makes the ink smear), more expensive per page and less crisp than laser printers.

Decent color ink jets can be found for as little as $75 and for as much as you're willing to pay. You'll probably want a color printer over just black and white. There isn't much difference in price.

Two things determine how crisp their product is: the number of dots per inch printers can print (d.p.i.) and the software that determines how those dots will be arranged. Shoot for the highest d.p.i. in your price range.

Software is another matter; it's hard to tell the difference between brands unless you can see them print. Ask sales clerks to print a sample page.

In general, Hewlett-Packard, Epson, Lexmark and some Canons are common and have done fine jobs on a variety of magazine comparative tests. (A warning: Lexmark printers, though they have the highest print quality in many tests, also have the highest costs per page for ink.)

If you're deciding between two models of similar print quality and price, consider two additional factors: warranty and speed. Most ink-jet makers guarantee parts and labor for at least a year. Make sure you have somewhere convenient to return the unit. Most printers don't have on-site service guarantees, and you might not be able to return it to the store where you bought it after 30 days (or less) have passed.

Be aware that the speed estimates for printers — measured in pages per minute, or p.p.m. — are usually based on so-called draft mode. That setting uses less ink, which is great for rough drafts, but it's also quite a bit faster than the better-quality printing you might do more often.

Color printing tends to be slower than black and white, so consider the speeds for both.

SOME OTHER THINGS TO CHECK:

LOOK AT THE PAPER TRAY. The more it holds, the more convenient it is. See whether you'll have to hand-feed envelopes or whether you can just take out the paper and stick them in the tray.

CONSIDER HOW THE PRINTER USES INK CARTRIDGES. Buy one that holds black and color cartridges at the same time. And be sure you can replace the black ink separately from the color so that you don't waste expensive color cartridges every time you run out of black.

You also don't want a printer in which you swap black and color cartridges. Those printers try to create black in a full-color photograph by combining all the other colors, and it never comes out quite right.

FINALLY, DETERMINE THE LARGEST SIZE OF PAPER A PRINTER CAN HANDLE.

Many ink jets can do 8½-by-14-inch pages, but some can't. Expect to pay more if you want a printer that can do 11-by-17-inch paper or banners.

Laser jets have the same dot size and speed measurements as ink jets. Color laser jets are almost affordable — a decent one runs $1,200 — but they're not yet within the budgets of most home users. Black-and-white units of good quality start at $200-$250.

All-in-one machines, which scan, fax, print and copy at home, are a good compromise if you need all those functions and don't want the expense or the space problems that result from buying a separate device for each task. But most all-in-ones have lower print quality and slower speeds than individual units.

ANOTHER ACCESSORY YOU MIGHT WANT WITH THAT NEW PC IS A SCANNER.

Scanners allow you to make a digital copy of something and store it on your PC. That could be a photo you want to send someone via e-mail, a document you want to edit or even the front of a box you want to sell online. Scanners can also do copy machine-like duty when combined with your printer, allowing you to scan something and then print it out.

Look for a flatbed scanner, which will allow you to scan things that aren't single pieces of paper, such as books or boxes. The bigger the glass size, the better. Though 8½-by-11-inch is the standard for home consumers, you might want to scan something bigger someday.

Scanners are measured in dots per inch for their scan resolution and in bits of color. Shoot for high numbers in both: 600 by 1200 dpi minimum for average home use, 36 or 48 bits minimum.

Be aware that scanners typically have two dpi measurements: optical, or hardware, and enhanced. Optical is what the scanner can see with its little camera. Enhanced is the supposed resolution the scanner can make that picture look like by using software tweaking.

Get a sales person to demonstrate how well the scanner works. If you can't see the scanner work, expect to get better quality the more money you spend.

Cheaper models — as little as $30 list, and lower than that with rebates and promotions — will do fine if you want to scan a quick pic for Grandma. But they won't do very good color reproduction, and their lack of crispness might disappoint you.

In comparing two models, look at warranty and speed. If you're trying to copy a short stack of documents — your tax return, say — that few-seconds-a-page difference will add up.

Finally, consider how you will connect the scanner to your PC. Parallel port scanners plug into the port your printer uses in the back of your PC. The printer then plugs into the scanner. Your printer and your scanner must work together correctly, so be prepared to return the scanner if your printer starts acting up. Or, if you're feeling technically savvy, you can install another card in your PC that has another parallel port on it for $15-$25.

SCSI (pronounced "scuzzy") scanners plug into their own card in the PC. Typically, these scanners come with the cards they need, but check.

NEXT ON YOUR SHOPPING LIST IS A MODEM. Modems are now incredibly easy to shop for: Get a 56 kilobit per second (kbps) model that is v.90 compliant. That's the standard. Of course, if you're buying a new PC, it probably comes with that kind of modem installed.

You might get better performance out of a more expensive brand, but most decent modems cost between $20 and $60 now.

You'll have to decide whether you want your modem to be internal (inside your computer) or external. Externals are a little more expensive because of the cost of the case. Depending on the age of your machine, they might run a bit more slowly because of the speed of the port the modem is plugging in to.

If your TV cable system offers cable modems, you might want to consider one. Granted, most cable modem service runs $30-$40 more than your normal cable bill. But you'll have fast access to the Internet, you won't have to pay $15-$25 a month to a service provider for an Internet account — and you won't have to pay for a second phone line.

ADSL service, if it's available in your area, is another alternative. Just watch the start-up costs and monthly fees closely, including what it will cost you to buy the initial hardware.

ALSO THINK ABOUT THESE ACCESSORIES

STORAGE: New drives allow you to insert cartridges to store hundreds of megabytes at a time so you can back up your files easily. Iomega's Zip drive, for example, holds 100 MB per cartridge and can be bought for as little as $50 with rebates. See the section on adding storage for more details.

CAMERAS: Digital cameras and video cameras help you skip the scanning step altogether, snapping images in digital form instead of on film. They're good for sending images by e-mail or on Web pages and for video conferences.

DOUBLE MODEM: If you're buying a gift for someone with two phone lines, consider something a little more snazzy than a regular modem: the Diamond SupraSonic II, which, like others of its kind, uses two modems to link the lines together and double your on-line speed. It runs about $90 and can be set to automatically drop one line or the other — without losing your Net connection — if there's an incoming call.

KEYBOARDS: Are you buying for a heavy typist? Newer split and curvy keyboards are much more comfortable in the long run. The more expensive models include a touch pad, which lets you control the cursor with your finger. It's hard to get used to, but easy to enjoy. Expect to pay $20-$75.

CRASH PROTECTION: Probably the best thing you can give yourself or any computer owner is a little extra protection against electrical problems. Extreme power surges can fry your PC, and even moderate shocks can kill your modem. Protect both with a good surge protector or an Uninterruptible Power Supply (UPS, $75 and up).

Cheap surge protecting strips may not make it through more than one storm, though you'll never know their protective power is gone. Invest the $30-$60 for a better model and make sure it includes plugs for the phone line that runs to your computer.

OTHER GOOD GIFT IDEAS TO CONSIDER: a new joystick for that game fiend, about $20; a digital video camera for simple video conferences (jerky pictures, but cute), $50; a pen and touch pad system that lets you dump your mouse and write on-screen, $50-$135; a wireless keyboard ($100) or one that has programmable buttons to get you to your favorite Internet site with a touch, $30; or a smart, comfortable or trackball-style mouse ($25).

KID STUFF: West Bloomfield, Mich., accountant Marci S. Grossman recommends spending the $15 or so it takes for a so-called keyboard condom if your children use the machine. It's a flexible plastic or vinyl cover for your keyboard. If a child's juice tips over, your X key won't be stuck forever.

Julie A. Sikorski, owner of Computertots in Rochester Hills, Mich., suggests the wide range of add-ons made by KBGear (www.kbgear.com): kidBoard, the Pablo pad, SketchBoard, JamCam. All are extras that allow your kids to draw or photograph in real life and have their creations show up on screen. ∎

Buying a laptop

Notebook computers: They're cute, they're convenient, and they're easier to lug around than a desktop PC.

And they may tempt you, even if you've never owned a laptop. Though portables can cost twice as much as a desktop PC, their prices have been plummeting.

But to buy the one that's right for you, shop carefully. Laptops are more expensive to upgrade than desktop PCs, so you'll want a machine that will suit you for as long as you intend to keep it.

How long is that? Ask yourself: Will you upgrade the software soon? If you upgrade software often, spend less on your laptop now. Buy something that will run what you need and replace it as it becomes obsolete. If, on the other hand, you're happy with the programs you have now, buy a more expensive machine.

"You're going to live with that machine for years, so make sure you spend money for quality," says Timothy Hopkins, Webmaster of Bubba's Web Design in East Lansing, Mich.

Once you've made that decision, consider:

THE BRAND: Sandy Kronenberg, chief executive officer of Defrag Inc. in Farmington Hills, Mich., and others recommend that you stick with brand names. IBM, Gateway, Dell, Toshiba, Compaq and others have good repair histories.

THE SPEED: Laptops are never as fast as desktop PCs because the processor chips that run them are designed differently. So don't expect the performance from a Pentium II 450 laptop that you would get from a Pentium II 450 desktop.

You'll likely choose among Intel Pentium models. Plain Pentiums (also called Pentium MMX for their multimedia capabilities) are slower than Pentium IIs, which are slower than Pentium IIIs.

Some lower-priced laptops may come with AMD K6-2 processors. These tend to be as fast as comparable Pentium II models on everything but 3D games that aren't written to take advantage of them.

Processors are also identified by clock speed, the number you see after the identification of the chip. The higher the number, the faster the chip. Don't expect to replace the processor later; it's a lot harder to make those swaps on a laptop.

THE SCREEN: Notebooks have active matrix or passive matrix screens. Active matrix screens are brighter, easier to read, crisper and viewable from wider angles — and they're more expensive. Screens are measured diagonally. Turn on the machine before you buy it to make sure the picture goes all the way to the edges of the screen. Some don't. Compare their prices against machines with smaller screen sizes.

In the fine print, look for the contrast ratio. This measures how bright the brightest areas are compared with the darkest areas. Your bottom limit should be a ratio of 35-1 or 40-1. IBM's ThinkPad 770Z has a ratio of 100-1 — excellent contrast. Dell's Inspiron 7000 series has contrast of 250-1.

Also consider the maximum resolution: The higher the number, the crisper the display. Your minimum should be 800 x 600.

THE MEMORY: RAM happens to be an easy upgrade for a laptop, but you should get at least 32-64 megabytes up front (128 in higher-end models). It's more likely to give your notebook a boost than buying a slightly faster chip.

Having more memory saves battery life, our experts say. It reduces the time your computer has to use the hard drive for temporary storage.

Speaking of hard drives, buy as much as you can afford.

"It's usually very expensive to upgrade these later," says Dick Minnick, senior technical specialist for Ford Systems Integration Center.

THE CD-ROM/DVD-ROM DRIVE: Some laptops force you to switch out the floppy drive and the CD-ROM drive so you can't use both at once. That can be inconvenient, but it's probably not reason enough to reject a system you like.

"I yearn for a unit that has both floppy and CD-ROM mounted in the case. I end up carrying both around in the bag, and the wrong one is always in the machine," Minnick says.

THE MODEM: Every laptop you buy now should have a 56 kilobit-per-second modem, even if you have to buy it separately. They're just too useful for doing everything from checking your local library catalog to sending in that information you just typed into another computer. (Do be aware that like desktop modems, laptop 56K modems will not give you true transmission rates of 56K because of technical limitations.)

Consider: Is the modem built in or is it a plug-in PC (formerly PCMCIA) card? Built-in is better; it keeps your slots free for things like additional storage devices.

THE PORTS: Some notebooks allow you to plug in only one device, such as a separate monitor or mouse, at a time. Others have a plug for every occasion. Make sure you have enough ports for every device you might want to run.

An alternative is to use a docking station, a box you put your laptop in that hooks into a traditional keyboard, mouse and monitor, making it almost the same as a desktop PC. The docking stations and peripherals can cost almost as much as a regular PC, so price them carefully.

THE POINTER: People quickly develop love-hate relationships with the mouse substitutes built into laptops. They fall into three categories: a stick you push around, a trackball built into the case that you roll or a touch pad that you trace over with a finger.

"If you have large hands, like I do, touch pads take a bit of getting used to, but are much easier to use than the eraserhead devices," says John Levis, owner of John E. Levis Associates in Livonia, Mich., a digital research firm.

Take some time to try the pointing device before you buy.

"Too often, I have seen people grow to despise that touch pad or trackball," says Tonya Thomas, computer trainer for Kappa Beta Computer Solutions in Detroit.

THE KEYBOARD: Play with this, too, testing that the size, angle and action — how the keys feel when you press them — suit your tastes.

Neil Jackson, president of Madison Communications in Dexter, Mich., says he's on the lookout for a laptop now "to give my work some legs." One of his top priorities? "A keyboard that is made for real people instead of munchkins."

THE BATTERY: Laptop batteries' charges last between two and four hours, which can seem terribly short when you're stuck in an airport. If you know you're going to be on the road a lot, spring for a spare battery. Otherwise, weigh the black box on the power cable that plugs into the wall, because you're going to be hauling it with your notebook.

"Check out the battery carefully," advises physician's assistant and laptop aficionado Jack Kircher of Essexville, Mich. "They always seem to exaggerate about how long the battery lasts."

THE BACKUP: The last bit of advice is from Alan Jackson, professor of computer and information services at Oakland (Mich.) Community College: "Make sure you have a readily available means of backing up the laptop. Do it once a day or at the very least once a week." He recommends a magnetic cartridge drive, such as Iomega's Zip drive.

Backups are important not only because laptops break easily (magnesium and other metal cases tend to last longer than plastic) but also because they're frequently stolen. Your insurance may replace the machine, but the data will be gone. ■

Palm-top computers & organizers

If people can't be too rich or too thin, then computers can't be too small or too fast.

At least that's the logic behind the growing pile of so-called palm-top machines that are filling the shelves of computer stores. But can they do the job?

I worked with five itty-bitty machines and one the size of a legal pad to find out. As it turns out, the one that I carried around and began to consider indispensable was not the fastest — or even the smallest — of the bunch.

There are several types of micro-computers, and the differences explain why prices and capabilities vary.

Palm-tops are typically about half the size of a notebook, or laptop, computer. They won't run Windows 98. Instead, they have a scaled-down operating system such as Windows CE, which can run simplified versions of Microsoft Office programs (Word, Excel and PowerPoint) and some other basic remakes of popular Windows programs.

They don't have desktop-style Intel chips, but instead rely on models made especially for palm-tops. Most palm-tops don't have traditional hard drives, but use chips to store information.

Their screens are tiny, and their keyboards almost an afterthought. But palm-tops (and organizers) make up for some of that problem with touch-sensitive screens. Instead of using a mouse or touch pad to scroll around your program window, you use a tiny pen (or, in a pinch, your fingernail) to tap right on the screen.

Organizers are smaller still. They have limited memory (2 to 3 megabytes is the typical maximum), use a touch screen or limited command buttons instead of a keyboard, and usually come with their own special operating system.

Many people use palm-tops and organizers as a bridge for their desktop PC. They take down information while they're on the road, then transfer that data back into their desktop computer when they return.

So I took a look at one more product that attempts to leap that gap: the CrossPad, manufactured by a division of the pen company, which digitally records notes that you make on legal pads so they can be transferred to your PC.

I looked at three palm-top models that run Windows CE, have bright,

touch-sensitive color screens and have a standard suite of CE-capable software: the NEC MobilePro 750C, the Hewlett-Packard 620LX (now being replaced by the 660LX) and the Sharp Mobilon HC4600.

(NOTE: Although these models have been replaced by more recent versions, the palm-tops you'll find on the market today share the characteristics of their first-generation brethren. So read this overview, check out what's available, and keep in mind the benefits and shortcomings discussed here. They'll still apply to the tiny computers you buy today.)

I had high hopes for these models. They have the traditional software (although it is a bit scaled down), they're lightweight, and they have a few fun extras. Two out of three, for example, have built-in voice recorders that let you use them even when they are turned off and closed.

But I quickly discovered that using these machines was not as much fun as I expected. They're heavy enough to be noticeable, and their size (between a paperback and a hardcover book) makes them impossible to stuff into a small purse, though they fit in a briefcase.

Using the touch-sensitive screen was easy. I wish they built regular laptops this way, instead of making us rely on awkward mouse substitutes. But all three machines shared a major handicap: their tiny keyboards.

This doesn't seem like a big deal until you realize how much typing you really do on a portable computer. Being able to type is part of what makes portable computers useful in the first place.

It wasn't long before I started leaving the palm-tops behind in the office and just carrying the organizers around. I tested two: the ultra-popular Palm III by 3Com (now replaced by the Palm IIIe, the Palm IIIx, the Palm V and, in some parts of the country, the Palm VII) and the RexPro (now replaced by the REX-3).

Both are designed to keep track of your address book, to-do list and memos on the road. The Palm offers thousands of programs ranging from a Web browser to a basic database program that can be loaded on it by using your traditional PC. Attachments like the modem hang off the outside of the machine.

You've probably seen a Palm III or its ancestor, the PalmPilot, without realizing it. It's a small gray block a little larger than a deck of cards covered with a touch screen and a few buttons. The newer versions, which come with a flip-up cover of gray plastic, bear a striking resemblance to an oversized "Star Trek" communicator: Scotty, beam up my appointments.

The RexPro isn't so versatile. It runs just the tiny programs that come with it, but its advantage is its size. The Rex is literally the size of a credit card, and it easily fits into a wallet. If you already have a laptop, the Rex fits right into the PC card slot when you want to trade information. For a desktop PC, there's a small cradle for the Rex when you want to connect.

I loved carrying both machines around and having instant access to phone numbers and memos. Each has advantages beyond your ordinary Day Runner: the RexPro's is its size; the Palm III's is the suite of software you can run.

The third bridge to a desktop is the CrossPad, which did a fabulous job of digitally transcribing the notes I took, line for line, on a legal pad. It uses a special Cross pen, which writes in ink just like a fine ballpoint, while simultaneously transmitting what you're scribbling into the CrossPad memory. The CrossPad itself acted like a clipboard for the pad, which was just an ordinary legal model from our supply room.

The only hitch here was my writing: The IBM Digital Ink software that comes with the pad had hit-or-miss results as it tried to translate what I had written into typed text. People with good penmanship would probably fare better.

Despite the better capabilities of the palm-top machines, I found the organizers to be more practical. When I want to use big-time computer programs, I want a big-time computer keyboard and would be much happier with a laptop. But when I don't want to lug a notebook computer around, organizers do a great job.

And the one of all these machines that I found indispensable? The Palm III. I liked it so much that I didn't send back the demo unit; I bought it. (See the software section of this book for nifty things you can do with your Palm organizer.) ■

Leasing vs. buying

The ads are as tempting as any new car come-on: Lease a new computer for $50 a month with nothing down.

But take a second look at the cash you'll pay before you sign. Most lease deals are bad investments, forcing you to pay much more than you would if you just bought the machine.

Take a recent lease deal Dell offered on one of its machines, which had a list price of $1,699. For a two-year lease, the payments were $84 a month; on a three-year term, they were $64. In either case, there were virtually no up-front costs.

But by the end of the lease term, you'll have paid $2,016 (for two years) or $2,304 (for three years) for a PC you don't even own. That's the equivalent of taking out a loan at an interest rate of more than 8 percent or 10 percent, respectively. You could float that purchase on a high-interest-rate credit card for a few months before things added up.

Leases may be worth it for businesses that have to replace their hardware every couple of years.

They're even worth it if you have to have a PC — and no, I can't think of too many cases where that would be the case — and have no cash to pay for it.

But for normal folks, it's simple: Just save a bit and buy it. ■

Buying used

You want a computer, but lack the cash.

Not surprising. Even so-called affordable PCs hover around $600. That's a chunk of change.

The alternative: Buy used. I know, computers are scary enough fresh out of the box. But by buying used, you'll have enough left over to eat at night. Most computers die within the first 30 days if they're going to die at all, so a computer that's been running longer than that is usually reliable.

To get an idea of what some older models are going for, check out one of my favorite used-computer trading services: Advantage Computer Exchange, **www.computerpricing.com**.

Then open your Free Press classifieds, your local shopper or even Web pages from folks in your area (try **www.alldetroit.com** for a list) and look for the machine you want.

A few tips:

If something's going to break, it's the monitor. Printers, especially old Hewlett-Packard models, are legendarily reliable. (Mine is a giant industrial machine from the late '80s.)

With monitors, make sure that colors are bright and that the screen doesn't show major distortion, lines or a dominant color (like pink or green). These are typically NOT economical to fix.

If you're worried that the inside is coated in junk, ask the seller to open the box. Some dust is normal, but something that looks like a bird's nest should make you think twice.

Make sure you can still get parts. Do a little research on the phone or on the Internet. Check the manufacturer's Web site or customer service line to see what the model came with. Then find out whether that type of RAM or those hard drives are available. Beware of machines like many in IBM's original PS/2 series, which required PS/2-specific RAM, drives and even modems.

Don't buy too old. A 486 may be a great deal, but it won't run Windows 98. You'll be locking yourself out of most of today's programs. Shoot for at least a Pentium. If you can't afford that, try for at least a 486, which will run Windows. And don't forget used Apples. Although they may be hard to find, they'll often run newer Mac software with some upgrading.

Never, ever buy a PC without seeing it run and using the mouse, keyboard, printer and anything else it comes with. Don't be satisfied with watching the current owner use it.

Spring for some extras once you have the old machine, especially a fast modem (56K), which should cost $50-$75. Be sure that the modem will work with your older model. One other cheap, effective upgrade: more RAM. It's not too expensive to plug in 64 megabytes, enough to run most older software, and it will greatly speed up your PC's performance. My favorite mail-order place for RAM: Mushkin, at **www.mushkin.com**.

Finally, buy a name brand. You don't want a machine from a company that's long out of business. ■

What to do with your old machine

An old computer is like an expensive dress that no longer fits: It sits in the corner and inspires guilt, but it cost so much you're reluctant to just throw it away. Every year, I get a flood of calls from people with old computers.

They wonder whether someone somewhere might be able to use their old machine. They've bought a shiny new PC, and their old one has become a giant paperweight.

Donating computers works like any other contribution tax break, though how much you can deduct depends on the fair market value of the machine. That's why many of us attempt to donate old computers when they're near the end of their useful lives. Sometimes even that can be a challenge. Charities are getting pickier about which models they'll take.

Start by figuring out the real value of your PC. Charity donations of used goods are based on the resale value. To get an idea of what that old PC is worth, visit a pricing index such as **www.computerpricing.com**. If your computer is worth more than $25 (don't laugh, because some aren't), get an itemized receipt from the agency where you donated the machine. That slip is your proof of having given it away.

If you're particularly meticulous in your dealings with the Internal Revenue Service, you might print out a copy of the used-computer price list that relates to your machine. Because those prices change from day to day, you want a record of what your computer was worth at the time you donated it, not next April 15.

So where do you donate your machine?

If you're in the Detroit area, start with Think Detroit and Americorps*VISTA's Team TECH, who cooperate in taking newer PCs and donating them to social service agencies. Call Think Detroit at 313-833-1600, 8:30 a.m.-5 p.m. weekdays.

Ask the community agencies you deal with regularly whether they can use a PC. Many churches and schools are looking for newer computer hardware to help with administrative tasks or to put together a lab for the center's children.

If your PC is too old for the agencies you call, don't forget about traditional charities that take used household goods. The Salvation Army and the National Children's Advocacy Center take more than just couches and old dishes; they'll haul off your old PC, too.

You can get information about some other agencies in the National Directory of Computer Recycling Programs at **www.microweb.com/pepsite/Recycle/recycle_index.html**.

Also check out Computers 4 Kids, a national program on-line at **www.c4k.org** . ∎

Adding on

Adding more memory

Many people who wonder whether they should buy a new computer really just need to give their machine a little more thinking room. These days, you can't do much without memory.

Computers use RAM, or random-access memory, to do their heavy pondering. Whenever you ask a computer to solve a problem (such as moving a paragraph or adding some numbers), it transfers all the information it needs into its RAM.

Think of it this way: When you get ready to do your taxes, you probably collect all your receipts in one place. The tabletop becomes your version of RAM: a place to store everything you need to handle the task.

Whenever a PC runs out of RAM space, it starts using the hard drive, swapping the pieces it needs in and out of RAM. It's what you would do if you couldn't fit all those receipts on the table: You'd file them carefully away in your file cabinet. Or if you're like me, you'd sweep them all into shoe boxes.

Either way, it takes a lot longer to find what you need, and that's why your computer slows down — quite a bit — when you run out of RAM.

Fortunately, adding RAM is one of the simplest upgrades you can do.

On a PC, pop the cover and look inside: In addition to the long, envelope-sized plastic cards that run things like your monitor and your modem, you'll see several business-card-sized plastic pieces with chips.

These are SIMMs or DIMMs, high-tech acronyms that really mean "plastic pieces with chips." Each of these RAM holders snaps into a slot, and your first task is to see whether there are any empty slots.

If not, you're going to have to rip out some of what you have now to install cards that have more RAM. (OK, if you must know, SIMM stands for "single in-line memory module"; DIMM means "double in-line memory module.")

If you do have openings, count how many slots you have. Some older Pentium PCs require you to install two identical SIMMs at a time, requiring two spaces. DIMMs can typically be installed one at a time.

Now you need to know what kind of cards you need. SIMMs and DIMMs have different numbers of pins, which are the little gold- or tin-colored leads on the card that form the connection when you plug the card into the slot. Some older PCs use SIMMs with 30 pins and some use SIMMs with 72.

In addition, PCs have two types of SIMMs: parity and non-parity. The difference lies in how the little cards communicate with the PC. Most computers these days use non-parity SIMMs, but it's worth a check of your computer's manual or a call to its support line to find out for sure. The manual is also the place to get an exact description of the type and speed of SIMM or DIMM you need.

When you've got these specs, buying the cards is a snap at your local computer store or by mail. Many RAM upgrades cost less than $50.

Most SIMMs and DIMMs come with installation instructions, so check the package. To install the cards, look at the ones that are already in your PC. To put in a new one, you'll usually slip it into the slot, then push it into place.

You may have to slide the new ones into the slot at an angle, then push them upright until they snap into place. Some DIMMs have tiny clips at each end; just pushing the card into the slot causes them to snap shut. And other SIMMs require you to put the cards in straight, then push them over at an angle. Your computer's manual, the position of the existing cards and the instructions that came with your new ones

will tell you for sure.

Once they're in, you're done. There's no software involved, and your computer should recognize that the new memory is there the moment you turn it back on.

Mac DIMMs work much like those in PCs, but you don't usually have to worry about installing them in pairs or buying parity memory. Check with your computer store or your owner's manual if you're unsure of what type of memory will work. ■

Adding a modem

If your connection to the Internet crawls or you're thinking about hopping on-line for the first time, you may be a candidate for a new modem.

With the new 56-kilobit-per-second models dropping below $50, it's an affordable upgrade to do. If you haven't bought a 56K modem yet, there's one thing you should know and two questions you should ask:

You should know that 56K modems don't really transmit 56 kilobits (about 1,400 words of text) a second. The maximum they can hope for, because of technical limitations, is about 48 kbps while downloading information into your computer and 33.6 kbps for whatever you send upstream. In real life, that's usually limited even further by the quality of your phone line.

"Many computers now come with a 56 kbps modem, theoretically capable of downloading information twice as fast as the older 28.8 modems," said Timothy Hopkins, Webmaster at Bubba's Web Design in East Lansing, Mich. "Of course, being a human, I'm theoretically capable of running as fast as Barry Sanders. Don't you believe it."

So although the new modems are faster than earlier models, don't expect the blazing speed of having, say, a fast digital phone line.

The first question you should ask before buying a 56K modem is whether it's compatible with the v.90 standard or whether it can be upgraded free. The v.90 standard is a protocol, or set of rules, that allows 56K modems of different types to talk to one another when you're on-line. The company that makes the modem should be able to tell you. Most modems these days are compatible with v.90, but it doesn't hurt to check.

Second, you should ask your

Internet provider (your on-line service company) whether its local dial-up number will support v.90 and your new modem. Again, most will, but some smaller providers haven't upgraded their older modems to the v.90 standard. You'll be able to connect to them at 56K speeds only if you have a modem that's of the same type as theirs. Older protocols include K56flex, which was used primarily by Lucent and Rockwell-type modems, and x2, used by 3Com/U.S. Robotics models.

It's important to obtain the same type of modem as your service provider if it hasn't upgraded to v.90 yet. (Your new modem will support both the older protocols associated with that brand and v.90, so you're set.) If you buy without asking, you may find yourself in a quandary: Your 3Com modem won't talk to your on-line provider's Rockwell-based model, or vice versa. For the short term, you're better off buying the model that your provider will support.

Here's how to install a modem:

First, decide whether you want your modem on the inside or the outside of your machine. External modems plug into a spare serial port on the back of your machine and are a bit easier to install. Internal modems are cheaper, plug into a slot inside your machine and don't take up any extra desk space.

If you buy an external modem, installing it may be as simple as turning off your machine, plugging in the modem and turning it back on.

Windows may immediately make note of the new device and prompt you to tell it what kind of modem it is. (Your modem will ship with a floppy disk or CD that has the necessary setup files). Or you can force it to add the modem by clicking on Start, then Settings, then Control Panel. Double-click on Modems, then click Add.

The modem installation guide will help you set it up correctly. All modems require two settings: a COM port number, which tells the computer where to send information for the modem to transmit, and an IRQ, or Interrupt Request, number.

All hardware on your PC uses IRQs. They're sort of like CB channels, allowing the devices to talk to the PC. Each piece of hardware must have its own IRQ, so the only trick is making sure that you don't assign an IRQ that something else is already using.

If you've got other devices (like scanners or cameras) using an IRQ you've assigned to your modem, both devices will start failing intermittently. Consult your installation guide to see how to change the IRQ on your modem and see whether that solves the problem.

If you're installing your modem internally, it's time to shut your computer off and pop the case open. Look for a spare expansion slot, the thin grooves that take those flat green envelope-sized cards inside your PC.

If you're replacing an existing modem, look for it now — it will have phone jacks on the end you can see outside the PC — and remove it.

Take your new modem card and plug it into an empty slot, applying firm downward pressure to get it to seat properly. If this is the first time you've used this slot, you may have to remove the silver metal tab that covers the back-of-the-PC opening for the slot.

That's it. Turn on the PC and see whether Windows recognizes the new modem. If it doesn't, go through the steps above under the Control Panel to add it. (This is also where you can remove your old modem settings if you need to).

To see whether you have two pieces of hardware trying to use one IRQ, try using the Control Panel: Click on Start, then Settings, then Control Panel. Double-click on System, then click on the Device Manager tab. Scroll down to the Modem section and hit the little plus sign to see your modem. If there's no exclamation point, there's no conflict. ■

Getting started with a cable modem

What if I told you that you could have Internet access at home that moved up to 50 times faster than a traditional modem for the price of a couple of meals out?

"There must be a catch," I hear you saying. And there is, both in terms of speed and security. But let's talk about the good news first.

Cable modems are available in most large U.S. cities, and they're spreading. If you're already a heavy Internet user and a cable TV subscriber, you can't beat the price: $40 to $50 a month on top of your cable bill.

Subtract your current Internet provider fee and the cost of a second phone line, and you've come close to paying for it already. And cable modems are continuously connected, so you won't have to dial in.

"I find that it has spoiled me, since it is so much faster than any dial-up service I used," said Rob David, a Northville, Mich., marketing consultant. "I'm a happy cable modem camper."

Call your cable company to find out whether you can get service. Depending on your company, you may have to use your phone line and modem to send information from your PC.

Now for the catch: You aren't alone in the fast lane. You'll be sharing your connection speed with the folks in your immediate neighborhood. Just as with automobile traffic, the more of you there are using the road, the slower you'll all go.

There's also a disturbing chance that the other drivers will be able to peek inside your computer.

If you've already set up your home computers on a network and designated some resources as being shared — things like printers and directories on your hard drive — those same resources will be available to anyone else in your neighborhood.

"I clicked on Network Neighborhood," Free Press reader Howard Kloc wrote. "Next thing I knew, I had 15 computers listed on my network and access to about four network printers.

"Scratching my head, I clicked on one of the listings and found myself looking at someone's C and D drive. I clicked on a directory and opened a .doc file. Seems that someone named Billy has just finished a school paper about going to the zoo over break. Can this be? Am I looking at someone else's computer? You bet! Cable users beware!"

George Booth, vice president and general manager of Comcast Cablevision of Detroit, said he'd never heard of that trouble, and representatives from several other companies said the same.

(**NOTE:** Cable company Media One contacted me after this column ran. It is aware of the problem and has added encoding to its system and has been educating customers on how to handle the issue.)

Tech folks have been talking about the problem for a while.

Theoretically, said Sandy Kronenberg, CEO of Defrag Inc. in Farmington Hills, Mich., a person on your loop of the cable modem network could use a so-called sniffer program to pick up all the packets of data moving over the network. The person could read your mail and every byte of information you sent out. Sniffer programs are depressingly easy for any junior hacker to download on the Internet.

But the chances of someone reading your mail or seeing what's in your computer are small — about the same as the chances that someone in your neighborhood is using a police scanner to eavesdrop on your older-model cordless phone. If you're concerned, make sure that you don't share resources on a home network if you're using a cable modem, or install a so-called firewall for protection.

For more information on firewalls, visit **www.zdnet.com/zdtv/search** and search for home firewalls. You could also look into Pretty Good Privacy (**www.epic.org/privacy /tools.html**), a basic encoding system that encrypts your outgoing messages. ∎

Adding a scanner

Just about everyone who owns a computer has thought at one time or another about buying a scanner.

These machines let you take a picture or drawing and turn it into a digital image. You can then send that picture of your kids to Grandma by e-mail, plop your car's mug into a For Sale advertisement or fax a cartoon to a friend.

Scanner prices are dropping — fast! — so it's a great time to buy one. Good models are available for $200. Cheap models can be had for $30.

Here's how to use one:

Many scanners plug into the port your printer uses in the back of the PC. Plug in the scanner, then plug in the printer. Install your software, and you're ready to continue.

Some scanners come with a card that plugs into the machine. Turn off the computer, pop the cover off, find an open slot next to the other green plastic cards that live in there and then plug the new card in. Put the PC cover back on.

Sticking out of the card on the back of the machine will be the data port for the scanner itself. Go ahead and plug it in, using the gray cable with big plugs that comes with the scanner. Don't forget to plug the power cord that came with the scanner into the unit and into the wall!

When you turn the computer on, one of two things is going to happen.

If you're running Windows, it may detect your new scanner automatically and prompt you for the diskette that the scanner maker gave you.

Otherwise, you'll have to use the maker's instructions to run that disk.

Once your scanner is installed, you'll probably be asked to reboot.

Most scanners come with basic software that allows you to scan simple pictures and save them. But many popular software packages allow you to scan right from that program. Popular faxing programs such as WinFax include a Scan and Send option, and most graphics programs allow you to scan a picture using the menu item Acquire or Get.

When you choose to scan a document, a window will usually pop up, allowing you to set some options. You can set the quality of the resolution — that is, how many dots per inch (dpi) you want to scan. You can pick whether you want to scan in color, grays or line art.

Remember, the higher the resolution, the more hard drive space that picture will take. A 4-by-6-inch photo scanned at 300 dpi can take more than a megabyte.

You will usually be given the option to pre-scan, or see what the scanned image will look like. This gives you the chance to select which part of the image you really want. For a photo, you won't

need to scan the whole letter- or legal-sized area the computer can capture.

After you pre-scan, a tiny picture of the scanned image will appear on the screen. You may crop the area that's scanned for real, and after you hit the Scan button, that portion will be scanned in more detail.

If you've chosen to Scan and Send in a fax program, the computer will now dial. You can save this new graphic on your screen to a regular file where you can get at it later.

A hint: If you're planning to send this photo to someone on-line, make it as tiny as possible so the receiver won't have to wait all day to download it. You can do that by reducing the color depth (the number of colors used to make up the image), reducing the size of the picture and reducing the resolution, or dots per inch. Finally, saving it in an efficient file format like JPEG or GIF means that it will be as small as possible. ■

Adding more storage

Your hard drive is full. Your backups take dozens of floppies or dozens of hours using a tape drive. It's time to look at removable media.

"Removable media" is geek speak for magnetic drives that let you take the disks out. Iomega's popular Jaz and Zip drives are excellent examples. You use them like a hard drive, then pop the cartridge out and stick another one in. Bingo! Tons of new space.

Jaz drives store 1 or 2 gigabytes of space per cartridge. Zip drives store 100 or 250 megabytes (depending on which model you buy). Either can be a big help in making backups of files or giving you more storage space. And they're so fast that you usually won't notice much difference between these drives and a normal hard drive.

The prices on these systems has finally dropped into the realm of ordinary folks. They range from less than $100 to $350. Jaz cartridges run $75-$100, Zips $10-$20.

This is more expensive than just adding a second hard drive, but it may be more convenient. The removable disks offer unlimited space because you can always buy more cartridges.

Jaz and Zip drives show up just like another hard drive in your computer's software.

They come in internal and external versions. External models plug into your computer's printer port, and the printer then plugs into the drive. External models are a bit more expensive (because of the necessary case) and slower than an internal drive, but they're convenient if you want to use one drive to carry information from one PC to the next.

Internal drives come in two flavors: SCSI (pronounced "scuzzy") and ATAPI/IDE. Most PCs use IDE controllers for their existing hard drives. SCSI is a bit faster, but it's not worth spending the money on an SCSI card unless you also plan to use it to run other hardware you'll buy later (such as SCSI CD writers or SCSI hard drives).

To install an external drive, plug it into the machine and into the wall.

If you don't like to muck around in your machine's innards, any computer service shop and some computer stores will install your new internal drive for you — for a price, of course.

Do-it-yourselfers, read on.

Installing a new Jaz or Zip drive on an Apple computer is easy. Mac drives generally already run on SCSI controllers, so you won't have to buy a separate SCSI card to use those types of Zip or Jaz drives.

To install the drive in a Mac, just find an open bay for it inside the machine. You'll plug a power cable and the flat SCSI ribbon cable in the back of the drive and make sure that the SCSI cable is still terminated — that is, there's some other drive or a big plug that ends the SCSI cable after your Jaz or Zip drive.

In either case, once you run the software that came with the drive, you're ready to go. For details, especially on figuring out how to terminate your SCSI cable, check out Iomega's instructions, which I found extremely easy to use.

Installing one of these drives on a PC works much the same way, except you'll be plugging the drive either into the flat cable that runs to your hard drive or into a plug on your motherboard. See the instructions for details. You'll also plug a spare power cord inside the machine into the drive. They look like collections of multicolored wire leading to white plugs.

If you choose to install a SCSI model, you'll have to plug in the card, then attach the card to the new drive with a SCSI cable. You'll have two sets of installation software to run: the first for the card itself, the second for the drive.

Again, the instructions on both the card and the drive are fairly easy to use, at least for people who feel comfortable working inside the machine.

JAZ CUSTOMERS, TAKE NOTE: Iomega announced in 1999 a recall of 60,000 power supply cords for the popular external Jaz storage drive because of a potential shock hazard. To see whether your drive is included, call 800-781-3296 anytime.

A QUICK WORD ABOUT CLICK DEATH: I've gotten calls from readers whose Zip magnetic cartridge drives (or their cartridges) have started suffering from what's known as click death.

Your drive starts endlessly clicking, and whatever cartridge is in it at that point is toast. Iomega, the maker of these drives, will replace cartridge or drive during the warranty period if click death occurs. See its Web page at **www.iomega.com/support /documents/2135.html**.

Some users say making sure you are using the latest versions of the Zip driver and Zip Tools (both available at **www.iomega.com**) may help avoid click death.

I still recommend these drives as a great alternative when backing up your PC; after all, floppies die, too. If something is essential, be sure to make two copies. ∎

Another storage alternative

The future of floppy disks is completely, undeniably dull.

That's great news.

Sitting on my desk is an Imation SuperDisk, the next generation of 3.5-inch floppy drives. It looks like a regular floppy drive, works like a regular floppy drive and sounds like a regular floppy drive: dull as heck.

In fact, even the floppy disks it uses look exactly the same. So why bother telling you about it?

Because these disks hold 120 megabytes each.

That would be exciting, if it weren't so easy to get used to. This drive could pass for a standard floppy drive any day of the week. It even reads and writes standard 1.44 MB and 720 KB PC diskettes. Using it is boring, easy and familiar: three things that are sure to make it an instant best-seller.

(NOTE: Technical squabbling among the people who created these drives and the incredible rise of magnetic cartridge drives have slowed the acceptance of high-density floppies. But they're still popular, and I suspect they will replace regular floppy disks at some point.)

High-density floppy drives are not just Imation products. (Imation is the diskette company spinoff of 3M.) Other brands are producing the LS-120 drives and their diskettes.

Here's how it works:

The SuperDisk uses floppies that have little designs etched into them. When you store information on the disk, a laser uses these designs to keep track of exactly where the computer is writing on the diskette surface.

This precision means that instead of fitting 135 lines of data in every inch like a normal diskette, the

SuperDisk can squeeze in 2,490 lines.

On PCs, the SuperDisk (and its competitors) can take the place of the standard floppy drive. It works exactly the same way, but holds more.

It also comes in an external version that plugs into the printer port on the back of your PC. Your printer then plugs into a port on the back of the SuperDisk. That's a little inconvenient: Besides being slower than the internal version, the external version doesn't allow you to print and store things on the SuperDisk at the same time. If you want to print a file on a SuperDiskette, you have to copy it to the hard drive first.

SuperDisks aren't as fast, internally at least, as their major competition: the Zip magnetic cartridge drive. But they do read standard diskettes, which makes them a superb replacement for boring old floppy drives. ∎

Adding a second hard drive

Your hard drive is full. You want another one.

You have a choice.

Option No. 1: Take your PC to a computer service center. Specify how big a hard drive you want and pay to have it installed. You're done.

Option No. 2: Do it yourself. Here's how:

Start by calling your computer maker's technical support people. They can tell you several key things.

First, does your computer use IDE or SCSI hard drives? This refers to the language they use to talk to your PC.

Second, is there room inside your machine for another drive? Ask them to describe where it could go. If you buy a 3½-inch drive (most are), will you need so-called rails to hold it?

Third, will your computer talk to a large second hard drive? Some old machines will ignore any second hard drive larger than about 500 megabytes.

Once you've got the answers, you can go to a computer store and buy a new drive using those specifications. It will become the D drive on your Windows PC (or show up as a second icon on your Mac). Your CD-ROM drive automatically switches to the next open letter.

Space is cheap these days. Just remember that every gigabyte of space holds about 300,000 pages of plain text. Graphics take much more space, with even tiny, rough, Internet-style pictures taking 100 kilobytes each. And new programs are horrible

space hogs. Office 2000 Premium, for example, sucks up 525 megabytes for a typical install.

When you get your drive home, read the instructions for installation.

But generally, you'll start by unplugging your PC. Then you open the case and identify your existing hard drive. It's a flat metal thing as thick as a paperback, with two cables coming out of it: a flat gray one and another with four multicolored wires. The flat gray one carries data. The colorful one carries power.

Check the directions on your drive. You may have to move a so-called jumper on the back of the drive to tell your PC that you're installing a second drive in the machine. A jumper is a tiny black plastic piece covering two metal pins.

On Mac drives, you may have a jumper for the drive ID and SCSI termination. See your instructions.

Locate the spot where the tech support folks said another drive could fit and install it there with screws. Plug a power cable into the back; there should be a spare one inside the machine.

On the gray data cable to your existing hard drive, there should be an extra black plug. Connect this to the new drive without unplugging the old one. Your drive is now installed. Plug your machine back in and turn it on. You'll see the computer identify the new drive, but you won't be able to get at it. Mac owners should fol-

low drive instructions to finish.

PC owners will need to format the drive. To do that, get to a DOS prompt. (In Windows 3.1, just click on File, then Exit. In Windows, click Start, then Shut Down, then Restart in MS-DOS mode.)

Type fdisk at the C: prompt. When you get the menu, hit 5 to change the active drive, 2 to pick your second drive and 1 to create a primary partition. It will ask you if you want it as large as possible; say yes.

Watch how big it makes that partition. Depending on the size of your drive and the version of Windows you're running, you may have to create second or third partitions, each of which will have different drive letters and will act like a separate hard drive (yet another good reason to upgrade now to Windows 98). Consult your manual for more information.

Otherwise, hit the Esc key to quit. When you get back to the DOS prompt, type format d: (and repeat this step for every new partition you have). This will make the computer format your new drive so that it can store information there. It'll take a few minutes. When it's done, so are you! ■

Hooking two computers together

As PCs worm their way into most American households, families are faced with a tough question: How do you make things efficient and save money when you have more than one computer in the house?

One way is to link those computers so that they can share information and resources. Linking the two machines lets you share printers, scanners or Zip drives. It may allow you to use a single Internet connection on two machines — even at the same time.

You may be using a network at work that connects your PC to others in the office. But a home network is typically much simpler: a single cable connecting two machines together.

You've got a couple of choices for connecting the PCs.

The cheapest is probably a Direct Cable Connection, said Ronald Draayer, head of the computer information services department at Davenport College in Grand Rapids, Mich. You're limited to two computers, and the cable can be only about 6 feet long before you start to lose data.

Faster and more flexible is a connection between two PCs with Network Interface Cards. These cost as little as $50 and allow a cable to be 150 to 200 feet long without problems. That's enough to run it under the carpet into another bedroom.

You'll end up buying two cards and installing them in your PCs; they usually come with software and instructions. Then you'll buy the appropri-

ate-length unshielded twisted pair cable with RJ45 plugs on the ends. (They look like phone jacks.) The good news about these cables is that they fit into network plugs that are built in to many higher-end PCs and laptops.

Be sure you buy the right type of cable; if you don't install a separate network hub, you need a cable with an extra twist, so that your cards don't burn each other out. Ask the folks who sell you the cards to help make sure that doesn't happen.

Setting up the PCs after you've stuck in the cards is simple. You'll have to decide what language Windows uses to help the PCs talk to each other; you'll find the different options in your Control Panel, under Network, then Configuration.

After you're set up, you'll select the items from each computer that you want shared on the network, whether it's a printer, a hard drive (or just one folder) or another piece of equipment. For instructions on how to do that, click on Start, then Help and then search for the key word "sharing." You'll see a number of topics listed that tell you how to share resources.

Another simple way to get this done is to buy one of the many basic network setup packages available at computer stores and catalogs near you. They include all the hardware you need and detailed instructions on how to get it going. They don't cost much more than buying the parts separately.

The bottom line: When you start your PCs, you'll be asked for a password. Once you type that in, it will be saved until the PCs are turned off again (or you choose to log off). You'll see the folders, printers and hardware you have shared on both computers.

Marci S. Grossman, a certified public accountant from West Bloomfield, Mich., points out the benefits of a networked connection: Two users can surf the Web together with special software. Or they can play games against each other. One PC can back up files from the other.

But she also notes the downsides. If you're trying to print from one PC and the printer is attached to the other, then that other machine is going to have to be on.

"I leave both of my machines on all of the time, having the monitors and hard drive sleep after a while so that all of my information is always available without waiting," said Jack Kircher, an Essexville, Mich., physician assistant.

For more information on setting up a Windows network, see: **www.zdjournals-.com/w95/9707 /w959772.htm** . ∎

Making CDs

The idea of making your own CD-ROMs is almost magic.

After all, CDs are what the software companies give you, not what you distribute yourself. There's something special about that shiny ring of plastic.

Fortunately, with prices for an internal CD-ROM burner dropping to about the price of a good CD player, you can own some of that magic at home.

Here's how:

A CD burner uses a laser to score the coating on a blank CD. Your information is recorded there in a fairly durable format.

Each disc, costs $1-$10, depending on where and how many and what you buy, and holds about 650 megabytes.

CD burners come in two flavors: CD-R and CD-RW. The R stands for recordable; the RW, for rewritable.

Be sure you know which you're getting when you buy a CD-ROM writer: CD-R drives cannot write over information you've recorded on a CD. You can write to a single CD until it's filled, and then you must start on a new disc. CD-RW drives let you erase and record over material you've put on a disc, and the CDs they create are still readable by people with ordinary CD-ROM drives. They don't cost much more than the CD-R drives because there's more of them sold and they are more flexible. CD-RW discs cost about $5 more

each than CD-R discs.

Recording is simple. Most CD writers include software that lets you drag and drop files from your computer onto a CD. If you're not sure your hard drive is fast enough to record smoothly — CD burners can be very picky about that — you can create a so-called disc image with your files.

That means the computer formats all the files to be written on the disc and crunches them together, making it easier for your hard drive to read them promptly and your computer to write them correctly onto the CD.

Still, you may experience a mistake every now and then while writing. It can be caused by anything from the hard drive speed to your accidentally bumping your computer.

The CD-R drive detects this and lets you know that your disc is bad. If you're using a CD-R drive, you're going to have to insert a new disc and trash the old one. If you're using a CD-RW, you'll likely be able to record over your mistake.

I don't advise CD writers for people who are interested only in making backups of the information on their hard drives. These CD drives take more time to record information than their faster magnetic cartridge brethren (like Zip or Jaz drives), and they're not as flexible.

But one trick a CD writer is great at: making copies of music CDs. If you've got a disc that has a scratch or is threatening to crack, this is one way to try to save it. ∎

Keeping it running

Making backups

A backup plan can save you days of work if something gets accidentally erased or your computer develops a problem. It can also be the only defense you have against losing information you don't have stored anywhere else.

Some of these tips on how to structure a backup plan come from Ron Davis, technical manager at the Data Recovery Group in Southfield, Mich. His company specializes in trying to recover information from computers that have crashed, gotten a virus or just broken down. His folks work on hopeless cases: data that have been formatted over or deliberately sabotaged or struck by lightning. But you can avoid visiting someone like Ron if you get into the habit of making regular backups.

First, set up your computer so that it can make copies of your important data. If you have a removable media drive, such as a Zip or Jaz or Syquest, you'll use its backup program to store files on those cartridges at regular times. Read your manuals for details.

If all you have is a floppy drive, you're going to have to make choices about what you save. It can take 2,000 floppy disks to back up a three-gigabyte hard drive!

Fortunately, most of the files on your computer are programs. If you still have the original disks you used to install the software, you don't need to back up those files because you can always start from scratch. So what you really need to save are copies of the documents, pictures and data you've created.

If you're running Windows 95 or 98, you have a backup program called Microsoft Backup. You can usually find it under the Start menu in Programs, Accessories, System Tools. Follow the directions to select which files you want to back up and when.

For your most important files, such as your checkbook or address book, take the time to back them up on a floppy disk that's stored separately from the program. The manual will tell you how to save a copy of these files to a diskette.

Davis points out that you can protect your work in progress, too. Many programs will allow you to automatically save changes every few minutes. For instance, in Microsoft Word, you can find this feature in the Tools menu, under Options on the Save tab. Read your manuals for details.

You can also save the file under a different name (usually by clicking on File, then Save As) to give yourself a second copy of it. You can put this copy on the hard drive or store it to a floppy disk.

Floppies are not terribly reliable, especially over the long run. Do not store information on floppy disks and kill it off the hard drive unless it's something you can afford to lose.

Never store floppies (or cartridges) near heat or magnets, including stereo speakers. The speakers on your PC have special shielding, so they won't erase data. Find a place for your disks or cartridges away from your computer, even in another building if possible. That way, if your computer is destroyed by fire, you'll still have good copies of your data. Do put them somewhere secure because your important files will not have the protection from prying eyes (such as passwords) they have on your computer's hard disk.

Don't always use the same disks to make your backups. If you back up once a week, use three sets of diskettes and rotate them. That way, if you decide you want a version of a document that existed three weeks ago, you won't have written over it since then.

Finally, test your backup to make sure you can retrieve files when you need them. As Davis says, "Right after your computer crashes is a really bad time to see if your backup system is actually working."

A good rule is to back up all of your important files once a week. For your most important files, consider backing them up every time you use them. Think of it this way: What can you afford to lose? ∎

Solving hardware problems

The smell of ozone in our home office was the dead giveaway — pun intended — that we were about to get some bad electronic news.

A nasty lightning storm had taken its toll on my computer. I was lucky because I had the machine on a fairly expensive surge protector. But even so, the strike was so close to our home (though, mercifully, not ON our house) that random devices quit working. Just little nonessential items like the modem and the printer.

Our first reaction, after opening some windows to vent the nasty odor, was to start checking out what had gone wrong. The PC had survived, and it worked perfectly. But several phones and the above devices hadn't. We immediately started troubleshooting what had been incinerated: cables, plugs, plug sockets, cards and boards.

What can you learn from this? First, that buying a surge protector is a smart investment. This strike was so close that some of our electrical outlets got fried and turned black. But several YEARS' worth of data, stored only on my precious machine — yes, I admit it, I was backing up only my checking account files — were left untouched because of my surge protector.

(NOTE: After this column ran, I heard from folks reminding me that the best protection during a storm is to unplug your machine, including the phone cords. That's great advice! Just remember that you're not always there to unplug the PC, so buy the protector, too.)

Second, the steps I took to figure out what had gone bad are useful any time you have a device that quits. Here's what I'd do. (I skipped the software step because I was pretty sure of what had killed my devices.)

Nine of 10 hardware failures are software-related. That is, the device is working fine, but the software has quit recognizing that the printer or modem or scanner or what have you exists.

Often, that's because some other program has come along and changed some crucial setting your device needs. This is why technical support folks' first question is almost always, "Have you installed any new software or devices recently?"

If you think it was a software problem, you can call the people who made your existing device. They may be able to help you identify the cause and solve it. If they can't help, try the people who made your new software or hardware and give them a chance to fix the damage.

Let's say you haven't installed anything new, everything is working fine and then something suddenly quits working. It's likely a hardware failure if it quits in mid-stride, such as a printer that dies halfway through a page.

If your machine is under warranty, by all means, return it to the store to get it checked out. But if it's not, start by making sure that the plug hasn't fallen out of the wall or that the cords haven't fallen out of the back of the device or the back of the computer.

If the cords are still plugged in, try wiggling them to see whether they may have loosened. If that doesn't help, try replacing them (if possible) with other cords from work or from home to see whether that solves the problem.

If the cords aren't the problem, the plug socket may be. Most devices involve two plugs: one for the device and one on the PC. If you can, try plugging another accessory (like a friend's printer) into the same plug on your machine to see whether the PC recognizes it. If it does, you know the plug on the computer is not to blame and it's time to take that device in to be repaired or replaced.

As a last resort, check out the manufacturer's Web site (often just www., then the manufacturer's name, then .com — such as **www.hp.com**). If there's a known problem with your device and an easy solution, you might find it there. If nothing else, you can probably find a list of stores that service your item. ∎

Questions about basic maintenance

It's the weekend, and while you're doing all that good house maintenance, you should take a few minutes to think about your PC. Here are some questions I get a lot from readers that might point you in the right direction when it comes to taking care of your PC:

Q: Should I turn off my computer when I leave the room?

A: Every time you turn your computer on, parts inside heat up and expand. When you turn it off, they cool down and contract. This cycle contributes to the wear and tear on your machine. But leaving the PC on all the time wastes electricity, and although computers have grown less temperature-sensitive over the years (remember those freezing computer rooms at the office?), that's still a lot of heat.

If you're leaving your computer for longer than an hour, turn it off. Otherwise, leave it on — you can always turn off just the monitor.

Q: What should I do about my computer during a storm?

A: Lightning, and the associated power surges, are your computer's worst enemy. Surges traveling on your electrical system can fry the machine, and extra ener-gy on the phone lines can toast your modem.

The best protection is to unplug everything during an electrical storm, including the modem from the phone lines. But you're not always going to be home when those storms happen, so invest in a good surge protector.

Q: Somebody told me to clean my keyboard and mouse, but I don't know how.

A: For the keyboard, turn it over now and again and give it a good whack to release all the dirt and dust that have built up inside. You should be able to unscrew the bottom of your mouse and remove the rolling ball. Wipe the ball gently with rubbing alcohol, let it dry and return it after cleaning out any other visible dust inside the unit.

Q: My printer is starting to print goopy pages.

A: On ink-jet printers, remove the cartridge and examine the bottom. Is it gunky? You may have gotten a bad one. If not, try swabbing out the area where the cartridge sits to make sure that there isn't a pileup of old ink there. If it's extremely bad, wet the tip of the swab with nail polish remover to loosen the dry ink.

Most laser printer cartridges come with a mini-cleaning kit. But if that's not doing the job, it may be worth the $10-$15 it takes to buy a real cleaning kit and give the thing a good once-over. Be sure to do this after the printer has been turned off for a while; the insides of laser printers get hot during use.

Q: My friend's computer just ate a bunch of his files. How do I keep that from happening to me?

A: Get any magnets off your desk. That includes refrigerator magnets, which never belong on your PC, but it also includes radios and non-computer-rated speakers. (The magnets in computer speakers are shielded.) Magnets can cause your hard disk and floppy disks to lose their data because that information is stored magnetically. Don't forget to always back up the files you couldn't live without! ∎

How to choose a repair shop

Suppose you discover your computer is inexplicably dead, without so much as a blinking cursor of a pulse.

Or maybe it's continuously hiccuping errors. Maybe it refuses to acknowledge that it has a mouse or a keyboard or a modem, no matter how much you check the plugs and wave things in front of the screen.

It's probably time for a visit to the repair shop. First, protect yourself. Most shops are honest and competent. But it takes only one bad experience to lighten your wallet and pull down your spirits.

Here are some steps you can take to make sure your problem gets fixed and no new problems appear:

Make note of the errors. If you're getting those dreaded screen messages before your computer fails, write them down, obscure numbers and all. They'll help the repair folks figure out what's wrong with your PC.

Don't take in anything that isn't absolutely necessary. Unless your problem involves an outside piece of hardware, don't take in cables, monitors or printers. Don't bother taking in boxed software, either. Even if you have to take in a printer or other accessory, don't take along the power or connection cables.

The more miscellaneous items that hitch along for the ride, the better the chances that one will be left behind at the repair shop.

Take a careful inventory of your system before you shut it down for the trip. Know exactly how much RAM you have and how big your hard drive is. If you have extra cards you've added inside, such as a modem or scanner, know how many there are and what they do.

Chances are, it will all be there and fine when you get the PC back. But if it isn't or if some of those parts had to be replaced, you want to know what you had to start with to make sure you're getting something comparable.

BACK UP YOUR HARD DISK. I can't emphasize this enough. You should be doing this on a regular basis anyway. If you have a huge drive and nothing convenient to back up on, back up on floppies the individual files that you've created.

You can skip the programs because you can reinstall them. But it's a smart move to back anything up that you can't easily replace. Inexperienced technicians have been known to erase perfectly working hard drives by accident — or the drive itself may need to be replaced. Either way, you'll be covered.

If you're having something specific done, get a firm price in advance in writing. If you're having a mysterious problem resolved, get a simple note from the technicians that they will call you if the repair bill will exceed a certain amount.

Find out in advance how long it will be before a technician starts work on your machine. The shop may not be able to tell you how long the repair will take if it's not immediately clear what's wrong, but it should be able to tell you how long it will be before someone tries to find out.

Get referrals. There is no better way to find a good repair shop than to ask folks who have had fixes done. Don't forget to call the Better Business Bureau to see if there have been any complaints. ■

Things that make computers fail

One minute, your computer is purring along. The next, it's snarling "illegal operation," hissing "general protection fault" or just playing dead.

You want to know why. Not just why it crashed this time, but why it does at all. If computers are binary machines that run on electronic components and a predictable string of 1s and 0s, why don't they ever work as advertised?

I got a glimpse of the answer when I sat in on an interview with Andrew Grove, then chief executive of Intel.

If you own an IBM-compatible PC, you've probably helped pay Andy's salary. His $25 billion company makes the processor chips that are the brains inside the vast majority of the world's personal computers. He talked about everything from what's coming in PCs to, well, why they don't work.

Here's the bottom line:

Intel wants more people to buy computers. To do that, Intel has got to make PCs do more. If what computers did now were enough, you already would have bought a machine, right? That's the reasoning.

But every time people come up with a new use for computers, it means there is a need for more power. Take multimedia stuff like games or video or CD-ROMs. Take the Internet. When these things got big and fancy, people took to them in droves, so the computers to run them had to get big and fancy, too.

Keeping up with customer demands keeps software and hardware companies churning out stuff as fast as they can design it, usually long before it reaches the reliability of your average kitchen appliance.

Grove said that if the computer industry stopped and perfected what it already had, PCs could be as simple as microwaves. The bad news: That's not likely to happen.

"If we thought that was what was the most important thing, that is what we would be doing. We don't," he said.

In any other industry, consumers could vote with their wallets by buying only simple or reliable brands.

But the guts of all PCs are strikingly similar. A few parts and software makers, including Intel, dominate the market.

There is no PC that will always keep its user free of hardware or software errors. And there's no way people can tell companies that they want more reliable PCs while at the same time falling prey to the more-is-better cycle. We've gotten so used to the trade-off — your PC does all the cool, new things, but you put up with a lot of

errors — that the only people telling computer manufacturers that there's something wrong with this system are the people who don't own PCs.

The message PC makers are getting from buyers is that power matters more than reliability.

Grove is certain that's the truth. However, for people who have resisted buying a PC because they don't think they are dependable, Intel is working on a simpler, more reliable machine.

Of course, it won't do as much, and Grove doesn't think people will really be satisfied with it for long.

He's right. Most PC users soon covet flashier models. Call it processor envy.

Meanwhile, continue to expect $2,000 PCs to crash, freeze and burn. Whenever you see your machine's final convulsions (from a "page fault" to a friendly picture of a bomb), just remember: This is progress. ■

Viruses

Friends, I have heard about possibly the scariest computer virus on the planet.

However — in the name of journalistic integrity — I have to tell you your chances of getting it are slim. And if you follow the suggestions here, your chances of getting ANY virus are slim.

Hackers with nothing better to do have exploited a weakness in Microsoft Word, and if you use Word to write your documents and Forte Agent or Free Agent to read newsgroups, there is a slim possibility that your private correspondence could end up published for all to see on the Internet.

Here's how the virus works:

Word stores a template for all new documents that tells it what font you want to write in, what your margins usually are and so on. Every time you open up a new file in Word, you're probably stuck in Times Roman 10 point — that's on the template. But a template can also store macros, which are recorded commands that play back when a new document is opened.

(For more on macros and how you can use them, see the software section of this book.)

When you open a document that has been infected by this new PolyPoster virus, it changes the template Word uses for all new documents. From now on, whenever you open a new file using Word, it runs a macro planted by the virus.

That macro, every so often, will cause your computer to attempt to send your new documents to Internet discussion groups. Your letter to Mom could end up on alt.fan.backstreet.boys, for example. Eeek.

Viruses that work this way are called macro viruses, and so far they've been created for both Microsoft Word and Microsoft Excel. This one works only if you also use the Forte Agent program to read newsgroups, so you're safe if you don't use that program or if you don't use Word.

Data Fellows, a San Jose, Calif., maker of anti-virus software, discovered the PolyPoster virus, but the company says the virus is extremely rare. I agree. I went on-line and searched archives of the newsgroups where this virus was supposed to post messages. I searched for the message subject headers it was supposed to use, but found no evidence that it has EVER infected anyone.

In fact, computer viruses are more rare than you might think. If you practice a few safe computing steps, you're nearly guaranteed to stay out of harm's way:

Invest in anti-virus software. This software scans all files for traces of viruses and gets rid of any it finds. Most newer virus programs also allow you to scan files as you download them and scan floppies when you stick them in your computer.

Be careful with floppies. If you accidentally reboot your computer with an infected floppy disk still in the drive, you could be giving yourself a virus at the same time that you see the "non-system disk" error. Scan all floppies from other folks with your anti-virus software and be sure there aren't any floppies in your computer whenever you turn it off or reboot.

You cannot get a virus by reading e-mail. You CAN get a virus if you download a file attached to your e-mail and run it. If you decide you want to risk it, download the file and then scan it with anti-virus software before running it. That goes for programs you see on Web sites, too.

If you have Word or Excel and want to protect yourself, check out **support.microsoft.com/support /tshoot/virus.asp**. Newer versions of both programs are designed to protect themselves against macro viruses, with varying degrees of success.

OTHER VIRUSES TO AVOID:

An attachment called **HAPPY99.EXE** has been circulating on the Net. If you download and run it or just run it from your mail program, you'll see fireworks and "Happy 1999!" on your screen. You'll also be infected with an annoying — but so far harmless — virus: Every message you send out will be duplicated, and the second copy will include the HAPPY99.EXE file, spreading the program further.

Don't run the program. Check the home page for your anti-virus software to learn how to get rid of it, if you've already run it.

MELISSA: This virus may be headed your way. It affects only people using both Outlook (the full version, not Express) and Word 97 or 2000. You get it by opening an infected Word document that's attached to incoming e-mail.

Melissa hijacks your system, send-ing a copy of that document to the first 50 people in your Outlook address book. It may also send out copies of future documents you create.

Do update your anti-virus software (free at the program's Web site). But, as software engineer Bernard Greenberg of Cambridge, Mass., points out, the best protection is never to open attachments you didn't ask for.

"If someone walked up to you on the street with a spoon of stuff and said, 'Hey, eat this, it's good!' would you?" he asks. "You'd have to be nuts, right? That's more or less what you're asking your computer to do when you execute a program you didn't ask for from an unknown or unestablished source." ■

When to do it yourself

You get a satisfying feeling when you upgrade or repair your computer yourself.

You pop the box and revel in your ability to identify most of the major parts inside. The ease of plugging and unplugging, installing and switching makes you glad you didn't hire a shop to do a simple job.

But how do you know whether the job you're considering is simple enough to do yourself? Take this quiz.

ARE YOU COMFORTABLE OPENING THE BOX?

YES: You're ready to do a RAM upgrade yourself.

NO: Better stick to add-ons you can plug into the back of your machine.

If you can get over the mental hurdle of opening the PC's case, a RAM upgrade is the easiest computer job there is. No software is involved, and the tiny cards that contain the memory fit into just one kind of slot on the main plastic board — the motherboard — inside your computer. Your PC's manual will tell you exactly what kind of memory to buy.

Once you've got it, all you have to do is open the case, identify the slots where the RAM goes and pop it in. It's relatively cheap, and it gives your computer a huge speed boost. This is a great way to start being a do-it-yourselfer. See the piece on adding memory in this section of the book.

ARE YOU COMFORTABLE RUNNING SOFTWARE TO INSTALL A NEW PART?

YES: You're ready to attempt installing a new modem.

NO: Stick to RAM and farm the other jobs out to friends or computer shops.

Installing a modem is probably the second-easiest installation you can do. Modems today are virtually all plug-and-play in the true sense of the phrase. You pop open the box, plug the modem into any open slot in which it fits, close the box and fire up the machine.

You're asked for the software that came with it — sometimes you don't even have to do that! — and the installation is done. For a discussion of some of the issues that may come up in an unusually complex installation, see the heading for adding a modem in this section of the book.

ARE YOU READY TO RUN MORE THAN ONE PROGRAM TO INSTALL A PART?

YES: You're ready to work with a scanner that requires its own internal card.

NO: You can still install simple drives (like IDE versions of CD-ROM burners or magnetic cartridge drives like the Zip or Jaz; see those articles in this book). Send the rest to the shop.

Scanners come in two flavors for PCs: those you just plug in your printer port and those that come with a separate card that must be installed inside the machine.

Pop the box, plug in the card, close the box, plug in the scanner and fire it up. You'll end up installing software for the card (usually it's just a SCSI — pronounced "scuzzy" — card, which can also control other types of hardware; see the articles in this book on adding storage), and then installing software for the scanner. After that, you're done.

ARE YOU READY TO WALK THROUGH A NUMBER OF SOFTWARE STEPS TO CONFIGURE A PART?

YES: You're ready to install a second hard drive.

NO: Stick to other types of drive installations. (You can handle CD drives or cartridge drives that require you to install a SCSI card). For a detailed description of the steps it takes to install a second hard drive, see the discussion of adding a second hard drive in this section of the book. If you can handle this, you're ready for almost any kind of drive installation.

ARE YOU READY TO SPEND SOME TIME TWEAKING YOUR COMPUTER'S SETTINGS (OR ON HOLD WITH TECH SUPPORT)?

YES: You're ready for most other jobs. Be sure to back up your important data first!

NO: No shame in sending more difficult tasks to the experts. Be sure to shop around. Video cards, sound cards and other parts that are used by many different programs in your PC can give your computer a performance boost. They can also mess up virtually every piece of software you

buy if they're installed incorrectly. Don't attempt them when you're on deadline for a project or when you desperately need your PC in the next couple of hours. ■

Calling technical support

Murphy would have loved computers.

If ever there was proof of the old saying that whatever can go wrong will go wrong, it's today's PCs. They're complicated combinations of hardware and software, all created by different people for different reasons, held together by a few technical standards and a prayer.

Which is a long way of saying that if you've owned a computer for longer than two weeks, chances are that some program you own doesn't work quite right, a piece of hardware is becoming a problem or you just can't seem to get things to work as the manual says they should.

You've read the literature that came with your PC. You've tried to work it out yourself to no success. Now it's time to call technical support.

You can make that call easier. First, figure out exactly which person to call. Some rules:

If something is wrong with your PC the moment you take it out of the box, call the PC manufacturer. It doesn't matter whether it's a hardware or software problem. That company is responsible for the setup of your PC as it's shipped to you, and the good news is that the wait on hold on PC makers' support lines can often be less than it is for smaller software or parts manufacturers.

If your Internet service doesn't work when you first get it, talk to the company that is supplying your service. It should be willing to help you get your software set up to connect correctly, even if it didn't make the program. (This assumes you're using the programs the company supplies or recommends to make your connection.)

If a program you installed AFTER you bought the PC goes wrong, it's time to call tech support for that software. The tech support folks can probably help you with conflicts, even

if the trouble stems from some hardware part inside your PC. Same goes for Internet software: If your connection is working fine until you install a new program and the program or the connection suddenly stops working, it's time to call the software maker.

If the conflicts crop up after you install new hardware (printers, scanners, additional memory, new drives), call the maker of the new hardware. Chances are that the new hardware is at the root of the trouble.

Once you know where to call, collect any evidence you need to describe the problem. Copy down the EXACT text you see in error messages. Describe on paper EXACTLY what sequence of noises and errors you're getting. If something quit working, what was it doing when it died? Were there any symptoms before it passed on? Find the software version (under Help, About if the program runs at all; look on the box otherwise) and the serial number of the item that's not working.

Finally, make the call. Or try the Internet. If your Internet connection is working, you can often get faster help on-line if you're willing to hunt for your answer. Virtually all software and hardware manufacturers have Web sites that include common problems, questions from other users and tips on how to use their products better. Try those sites first.

If you can wait for an answer, try e-mailing technical support rather than calling. You may get a more thought-out response.

When you do call, be prepared to

wait on hold. Grab something to read or a TV remote. Treasure the companies that answer your call promptly with a real human being; they're an endangered species.

Once you're on the phone, don't hang up until you have a resolution to your problem. By the end of the call, you should have fixed the trouble, gotten whatever authorization you need to return the software or part for a full refund or been referred to another technical support line that can help. If you have to hang up to test a solution (because your Internet connection uses your phone line, for example), try to get the name and number of the specific employee you talked to. At worst, get a case number that will allow other techs to see what you've already tried.

"I don't know" is an answer you should never accept. Ask to speak to a Level 2 support employee. Most tech support lines maintain a highly trained group of specialists for people whose questions are too complicated or bizarre for the front-line techs. ■

ONCE you know where to call, collect any evidence you need to describe the problem. Copy down the EXACT text you see in error messages. Describe on paper EXACTLY what sequence of noises and errors you're getting. If something quit working, what was it doing when it died? Were there any symptoms before it passed on?

Choosing computer books

Manual lawn mowers. Manual typewriters. Manual engine cranks. Even the word "manual" reminds us of effort, struggle, resistance. Is it any surprise that the hardest part of getting to know your computer is reading the manual? Open those covers, plow through that dense type, and you'll wish you were out manually mowing the lawn.

There are better alternatives. Books are written every year on nearly every type of computer hardware and software by people who actually speak English and communicate with other human beings more often than they talk to computers. You don't even have to walk into a computer store to buy them. Just visit your favorite bookshop. Most have a decent selection of computer books.

But once you get into the store, you'll quickly realize that the problem isn't finding the book you need. It's figuring out which book you need.

First, decide whether you're looking for a basic overview of a software program or an in-depth resource.

BASIC: Pick something like the "For Dummies" series, which is skinny and has lots of illustrations. (Don't worry. Many advanced users have "Dummies" books on their shelves.) It'll be easy and entertaining to work through from start to finish.

IN-DEPTH: Swallow hard and look through the thick tomes published by folks like Que and Sam. Que books are edited well, but there's a quick way to determine which reference is for you:

Think of a particular question you really want answered. Do you need to print labels of an odd size from your word processor? Do you want to learn about self-joins in a database program?

Flip through the books and see how long it takes to find your answers. I've bought computer books this way for years and have never been disappointed. Typically, if you can find the answer to your question quickly (and it's explained clearly), you're going to have an easy time finding the answers to questions you have later.

Don't worry that the books are too thick. You're not going to read these cover to cover. Instead, you'll use them like an encyclopedia to look up just the information you need.

Be prepared to spend some money. Smaller guide books, such as the "For Dummies" series, cost around $20. References, such as the Que Special Edition series, can run $45-$90.

If that's too much, consider these alternatives:

Visit a store that sells used books. Computer manuals, especially for the not-most-recent version of your software, do turn up and may be more reasonably priced.

Check out your library. Many libraries also offer free computer classes.

Hire a computer tutor. These folks, who usually come to your home, cost about as much an hour as the book would. But the instruction is geared to exactly what you want to learn, which may be more helpful. Find them in the classified ads, at your local community college or get a recommendation from your library or a computer person you know.

Join a computer club. Check your local community listings for computer clubs, or call local community centers. These are informal groups who have a general interest in PCs. Many offer meetings with speakers about different computer topics, and most have enough experienced members to help you get simple questions answered. ■

Y2K and your PC

Is your PC ready for the year 2000?

Most of the news coverage on the year 2000 crisis has focused on big government and corporate mainframes.

That's because those folks are going to have to spend somewhere between $300 billion and $600 billion to hire programmers to fix all the 1970s and 1980s programs they use that refer to the year in two digits. On Jan. 1, 2000, all those programs are going to think it's 1900. They're also going to think your phone bill is 100 years past due, that your credit card expired 100 years ago and that your milk's expiration date is 100 years old.

A good number of PCs will not recognize the year 2000 either or their operating system (DOS, Windows 3.1, even some parts of Windows 98) won't believe it.

Even if your PC itself makes it through 2000 unscathed, your software may conk out. Microsoft has acknowledged that a pile of its applications, including its popular Office 97 suite, have the year 2000 bug. Those software glitches are going to affect Apple users, too, even though the machines themselves will do fine.

But there is hope:

If you have a machine bought since 1998, you probably don't have to worry about your hardware at all. Same goes for software: Programs purchased shortly before the end of 1999 are less likely to have troubles. Office 97 isn't year-2000 compliant, but Office 2000 is.

To make a preliminary check of your PC, start by resetting the date and time to Dec. 31, 1999, at 11:59 p.m. (Exit all versions of Windows to the DOS prompt and type date, then Enter to change the date; time, then Enter to change the time.)

Next step: Wait a minute, then go back into the date and time to see whether they have changed themselves to 2000. No? Reset the date manually to Jan. 1, 2000, then turn the machine off and wait a few minutes. Turn it back on and see whether the date stayed

changed. If it did, you're fine. If it didn't, you need to call your PC manufacturer to see whether there's an upgrade for the BIOS (the bit of software that helps start up your PC) for your machine.

Next: Test your favorite applications. Put a record in your database or spreadsheet that has dates beyond the year 2000 in it and tell the program it's a date field. Then try to sort a column of dates with the 2000 in it.

Does the program put those records first, thinking they're 1900? Do the same with a fake check in your checkbook program. Does the program behave as if the check is dated 1900 or 2000? Also see whether your programs will accept 2/29/00, meaning Feb. 29, 2000; if the program thinks that 00 means 1900, it may reject that date since there was no leap day in 1900.

If any of this causes you problems, take note. Most software manufacturers are not offering free fixes to their products. They're expecting you to upgrade the entire program before 2000. That's not a great solution. But at least you know the problem exists, and you won't be surprised the morning after.

For more information, see the Year 2000 World Wide Web site: **www.year2000.com** or visit Microsoft's explanation of the problems its software will have: **www.microsoft.com/year2000** . ■

Y2K and Windows

Will your version of Windows survive the date change at the end of this year?

First, let's deal with a common misconception: Changing the way your dates are displayed in Windows (by going to Start, Settings, Control Panel, double-clicking on Regional Settings, choosing the Date tab and selecting m/d/yyyy in the Short Date Format drop-down box) does NOT fix the Y2K bug. This was a common urban legend on the Internet until it was unwittingly spread by a computer columnist in Florida, thereby guaranteeing its place in the rumor mill.

Changing the date in that way is a good idea, because it instantly alerts you to Y2K problems you may be having in other programs. You'll be able to see immediately whether a date is about to be recorded as 2014 or 1914.

But it does nothing to change the way Windows STORES the date, which is the origin of Windows' Y2K problems. It also doesn't change how Windows formats the date it sends to other applications that ask for it (though it will change how those applications display the date to you), so they'll continue to be messed by up Windows date errors.

If your version of Windows isn't Y2K-compliant, you'll have to update or upgrade. Sadly, no simple date-format switch will take care of the problem. So is your Windows ready?

WINDOWS 98 FIRST EDITION:
You'd think that because this product was released in late 1998, long after the hoopla started about the Y2K bug, it would be fine. Think again. You need the Y2K update, which Internet Explorer users can get at **www.windowsupdate.com** and others can get by calling 1-800-363-2896, 8 a.m.-10 p.m. weekdays.

After you install the update, Windows 98 is year 2000 compliant (or at least that's what Microsoft says). Check with the makers of your other software packages to make sure they're prepared as well.

WINDOWS 98 SECOND EDITION, which went on sale in summer 1999, already includes the Y2K fix.

WINDOWS 95: Let's concentrate on the original version (4.00.950, released in July 1995) because that's the oldest and most likely to have problems. Some — but not all — of these issues may have been fixed in your version of Windows 95.

To see which version you have, click on Start, Programs, MS-DOS Prompt. When the window appears, type VER at the DOS prompt and hit Enter. It should tell you exactly what you're running. Type Exit and hit return to get out of the DOS window.

Like Windows 3.1, which I'll detail later, the fixes that Microsoft offers for various 2000 problems with Windows 95 won't take care of everything. The program "remains compliant, with minor issues, with or without these updates," as Microsoft puts it. Microsoft has promised to post updates that will fix all Windows 95

problems before the end of the year.

Given some of the previous problems that Microsoft has considered minor issues, this language doesn't inspire confidence. I'd seriously consider upgrading to Windows 98 Second Edition rather than waiting to see what happens.

If you plan to stick it out, here's what to expect:

The Find results from your Start menu will give you funky creation dates for files made after the new year.

If your control panel is set to use two digits to identify dates, you won't be able to use Set Date/Time to correctly pick the computer's date. If you usually use the DATE command from a DOS prompt, that won't work correctly either, unless you type in four digits for the year.

Windows Explorer won't display file creation dates correctly or sort your files correctly based on when they're made.

The time and date window in your control panel will permit you to choose Feb. 29 even on years that don't have that day.

The phone dialer won't show the right dates for your calls in its log.

The programs you use may be affected by a slew of bugs that you won't see directly. But the results may be dates showing up as the early 1900s, or showing up as one day earlier than expected, or showing up as garbage.

WINDOWS 3.1: This version won't die altogether on Jan. 1, but you may notice some oddities that aren't fixable. You won't be able to manually set the date to 2-29-2000, for example, and you'll have to type in four-digit dates whenever you set the date and time in order for the system to work correctly.

Files created after the turn of the year won't display the correct date in Windows Explorer or in the file properties. The patch for this works only for Windows for Workgroups, or Windows 3.11.

The biggest concern with a machine running Windows 3.1 is that, because of its age, most of the software you're running with Windows will not be compliant with the year 2000.

Anything that depends on dates (your checkbook, when your caches expire in your Web browser, you name it) may be affected. And if your computer — the hardware — is equally old, there's a chance it won't recognize the date change correctly even if Windows and all your programs do.

GETTING HELP: Information about the problems and such fixes as Microsoft offers can be found at the Microsoft TechNet Year 2000 product site: **www.microsoft.com /technet/year2k/product /product.asp**.

Just scroll down until you see the Select Product box. Use the scroll bar on the box until you see your software, then click on it and click on Search. This site also has information about Y2K troubles with other Microsoft programs. ■

Software

The basics

Buying software

D o you want to start building that family tree, designing that back-yard herb garden or setting up the books for your home business? It could be time to make a trip to your local software store for a new toy.

To pick the best software title from all those look-alike boxes on the shelf, use these techniques:

Prepare in advance. The best place to learn about software is on the Internet. If you don't have access, most programs are expensive enough to make it worth a trip to your local public library, which probably has free Internet access terminals you can use.

If your library doesn't have Internet access, it may well have back issues of a computer magazine or two. Some of those have indexes, published in the back of the magazine or separately once a year, that guide you to the correct issue for the reviews of the software in which you're interested.

Once you're on-line, visit the software's home page and some review sites. If you're not sure what the main site is for the software company, you can try guessing by putting www. before the company name and .com after it, or by checking out the section in this book on finding Web addresses.

Many magazines have their software reviews on-line. Ziff-Davis puts its reviews on the excellent Computer Shopper site, which also shows you the prices for programs at various merchants. You'll find it at www.computershopper.com. Click on Software. (You can go directly to ZD's PC Magazine reviews by visiting www.pcmagazine.com.) Or try CNet at www.cnet.com and click on Software.

Another sneaky way to see how much people like software: Visit on-line auction sites like Amazon (http://auctions.amazon.com) or Ebay (www.ebay.com) and see how much people are willing to pay for used titles of the type you want to buy. Prices depend on three things: How recent is the program? How many copies are on the market? And most important, what's the word on the street about the quality of the software?

(You can pick up a program cheaply in auctions. Just make sure it's got the original discs, was not included as part of the original software shipped with a PC — that's illegal to sell — and is being sold by someone with a good feedback rating.)

Check the requirements. On the side or bottom of every software box is a listing of the basic system the program needs to run. If your computer is too old, or too slow, or incompatible, there's no point in considering the program at all (unless you're willing to upgrade for it). Remember that Apple or MacOS software can't run on Windows or vice versa, unless you've got special emulation software or hardware installed.

Take a moment to read the advertising copy and look at the screen shots. But take it all with a grain of salt. This isn't a thoughtful description of the program. It's a sales job. What you can get from looking at the box is a basic idea of the functions built into the software and maybe a picture of what the program's screens look like.

A note if you're buying games: Game software boxes often include still graphics from video cut-scenes in the program. That doesn't mean the game will actually look like those pictures during play. Pick the worst shot on the box. That's likely to be the quality of most of the production.

Ask around. It's fine to listen to what the computer store salesclerks have to say about software. But when they've finished telling you the features, be sure to ask whether they've used the software themselves and how often. Be skeptical of any recommendations from folks who aren't experienced with a particular program. ■

Finding free programs

Pssst, buddy. Want some free software?

On the Internet there is freeware, or software that you can download and use forever completely free of charge, and there's also shareware. That's software you use free until you are overcome by guilt and send in a tiny check (usually $25 or so) to the people who wrote the program.

There are demos: versions of commercial software that are either scaled down in features or set to quit working after a certain time. And finally, there are betas: early versions of commercial software that haven't had all the bugs worked out.

So how do you find all these goodies?

Shareware.com, **www.shareware.com**, with more than 250,000 programs, may be the best freeware and shareware site. You can search for software by key word and by platform (Windows 98, MacOS, etc.). Or you can just browse.

Searching for gardening programs at Shareware.com turned up two titles: a gardening journal and Green Thumb, a card game. Searching for "organizer" turned up hundreds of titles, ranging from software that catalogs coupons, music, collectibles or wine to programs that keep track of appointments.

Next is ZDNet's Hotfiles, at **www.hotfiles.com**. Ziff-Davis publishes a host of computer magazines, including PC Magazine, MacUser, PC Computing and Family PC. Hotfiles has everything from shareware mentioned in stories to programs that magazine editors and writers have written to a vast collection of shareware and freeware titles collected elsewhere.

The key word search is easy to use, and the Editor's Picks are a good way to browse.

Dave Franklin's DaveCentral, **www.davecentral.com**, wins the prize for best software site run by what seems to be an ordinary guy. There are a zillion programs. You can scroll through the most popular

downloads, check out new programs or browse for titles by subject.

Dave's key word search pulls up only programs that have that word in their title, which is limiting. But search results are easy to read, and the site has a fun, casual feeling.

Rocket Downloads, **www.rocketdownload.com**, also has lists of new and popular software, and it lets you scroll through subject categories. Its key word search results look clumsier than the top three, but there are tons of titles in the results. There isn't any way to specify which platform you want.

If you're looking for a new screen saver, there's really just one site: **www.screensaver.com**. This huge collections of useless animation is a monument to how much time we have on our hands.

If you're looking for more free stuff than software, take time out for the Free Site: **www.thefreesite.com**. It has a collection of free software by category and has additional categories for free samples, prizes and so forth.

Finally, there are two sites you should check out for additional links: Pass the Shareware, **www.passtheshareware.com**, has an awesome list of Web sites that have shareware or freeware available.

You can learn how to download programs once you find them, by reading the instructions in the Internet section of this book. ■

Getting rid of programs

"Hard Disk Full."

Seen that flash on your screen recently?

Hmm. Could be that travel agency program you loaded on a whim last week. Or maybe it's the 15 action games your kids don't play anymore.

The bottom line: You need fewer programs. But how do you get rid of programs once they're installed?

For both Apple and PC owners, the first step is simple: Check the folder the program lives in (and, in Windows, the software's program group) and look for an icon that says Uninstall.

If you find it, double-click on it and your program is history.

If you don't, read on.

APPLE USERS: Drag the program's folder and all its contents to the trash. Do the same thing for the program icon. Now you're done. Go have a cup of coffee and gloat.

IF YOU'RE USING WINDOWS 95 OR 98: Your next step should be to visit the Control Panel (Start, Settings, Control Panel) and double-click on Add/Remove Programs. If the program you want is in the list, click on it and click on the Remove button. You're done.

If not, or if you run Windows 3.1, you've got more work to do. And you have a choice: Do you want to do this yourself or buy software to do it?

CyberMedia's UnInstaller and Norton's CleanSweep (each about $40-$50) can eliminate unwanted programs. In my experience, UnInstaller is less likely to delete tiny program files you might need later, but CleanSweep does a better job of getting rid of every last trace. If you're not an experienced computer user, stick with UnInstaller.

The new versions of both programs don't work in Windows 3.1, but old versions are still available.

If you'd rather do the work yourself, here are some suggestions. Please don't attempt anything unless you're a knowledgeable computer user. It's fairly easy to delete something you might need later. Remember: If you're in doubt, keep it.

Start by getting rid of the program's folder and all its files.

Then look in the Windows directory (and the subdirectory System) for a file that starts with your program's name or abbreviation and ends in .ini. Delete it.

Click on Start, then Run (or in Windows 3.1, click on File, then Run in File Manager). Type sysedit and hit Enter.

Copies of all your system files will open on the screen. You want to look at four: autoexec.bat, config.sys, win.ini and system.ini. Scroll through them, looking for mentions of your program.

If you find any in autoexec or config, type REM at the beginning of each of those lines.

If you find them in win or system, put a semicolon and a space (;) at the beginning of each of those lines.

Save each file by bringing it to the front of the window, then clicking on File, Save. When you're done, close the System Configuration Editor by clicking on File, then Exit.

You're done. If you get errors when Windows starts up, it's because there are System Registry entries that refer to your missing program.

You can edit the registry by clicking on File, then Run, then typing regedit. But don't do it unless you have a good manual! ■

When software freezes

There's nothing worse than seeing a good computer go bad.

One minute it's humming away, balancing your checkbook or showing you that new Web page. The next, it's giving you repeated General Protection Faults, Illegal Operations or, if you're a Mac person, just the dreaded bomb.

We all want to know why this happens. Although I can fix most computer problems I encounter, many I can never explain.

Some programs just don't seem to like one another. Others must have been born under the wrong astrological sign. And some just refuse to get along with particular types of computers.

Whatever the reason, you're stuck trying to get your cranky machine moving again. Here are some tips to help you figure out how to fix what went wrong.

In rare cases, it's a hardware failure. But most of the time, it's something you've changed: a new piece of software that you've installed (or taken away), a setting you've tweaked or a new procedure you've tried.

This doesn't mean that you've done anything wrong. It just means that the change is disagreeing with your machine. That's why computer repair people look at you suspiciously when you bring your PC in for help, as if to say, "What did you do to it?"

If you can, change whatever you did back to see whether that makes the problem go away. If so, then you can call technical support for your software and sound knowledgeable: "Whenever I try to do XYZ, it crashes my machine. What's the deal?"

If you can't change it back, you've got two options: Call tech support to see whether someone there can help you make it work or reinstall the balky software. Be aware that if it's a setting that's been changed, you may have to uninstall your existing copy of the software before reinstalling it to get rid of the offending options.

Second, don't be intimidated by "protection fault" or "illegal operation" error messages. They're the computer equivalent of a burp. And although advanced A-level tech support people can decipher them, I can't, even after 19 years of using PCs. Do watch them to see what program is causing the problem.

But don't worry about deciphering all those numbers and letters.

Third, some errors occur because you ask too much of your machine. It's very difficult for your computer to run a DOS program in Windows, for example, although it will try. Seemingly simple things, such as printing, can actually take a lot of your system's resources. And every program you leave running in the background or minimized at the bottom of the screen is taxing your PC.

If you ask your computer to do too much, it may start spitting out random error messages. Close out a few things and try again. Speaking of which, tip No. 4 is a computer repair person's main technique: Turn things off and turn them back on again.

Shut down the program and start it up again. Shut down the PC and start it up again. If you're feeling lazy, try it more than once. This fixes about 25 percent of computer errors, as whatever got twisted up gets straightened out. And it doesn't require forking over money or waiting on hold.

If you're following the directions in the program manual and it just won't do what it's supposed to, stop and read those instructions again. Remember that computers are very literal: If you don't click in the right place and type exactly the right letters in the right order, your computer won't do what it's supposed to.

Sixth, be aware that you can get help. There are user groups for every major type of software on the Internet. They're often available right from the software manufacturer's Web page. That Web page may have frequently asked questions, which may include your problem. There are always aftermarket manuals in book stores, and they are typically written in something closer to English than standard computer manuals.

And finally, never be afraid to ask your friends. You never know: You may be able to solve their next problem. Whatever the cause.

So how do you handle the immediate problem of the error on your screen, you ask, so you can move on to the step of diagnosing what's wrong? Try these tips when ...

YOUR MOUSE POINTER DISAPPEARS. Don't panic. Try moving the mouse around to see whether the arrow reappears at the corners of the screen or down on the task bar. If you were having the computer save a file or do something else taxing, you might give the pointer a minute or two to return.

If it doesn't, try to save your work and reboot the computer with some keyboard shortcuts.

First, you can control the menus of virtually any Windows program just by tapping the Alt key once. Try it at a time when you're not having troubles. See how the word File is highlighted or set in a raised box? You can toggle through all the menus now by hitting the right arrow key to move over each word: Edit, View, etc.

To open the menu that's highlighted, hit the down arrow. You can now use the down arrow to move the highlight down to the item you want (such as File, Save), or just hit the letter on the keyboard that's underlined in the menu item you want.

If you have to fill out a dialogue box (to pick a file name if you're saving), use the Tab key to move between the boxes and buttons. When a button is selected, it will have a faint gray dotted line around it. To "click" on that button, hit the Enter key.

Once your work is saved, you can exit the program using this method (File, Exit). Now you want to reboot.

Holding down the Ctrl key, tap the Esc key. It will open the Start menu. Use the up arrow key to select Shut Down, or just hit the letter "u." To toggle the buttons so your computer restarts instead of just shutting down, use the Tab key to highlight Restart; then hit the Enter key to select it.

YOU GET THE BLUE SCREEN OF DEATH. This nasty blue screen is left over from the bad old days of DOS, and seeing it indicates that either a) your program has done something very, very bad or b) Windows itself has become unstable, striking out randomly at other programs.

You never have a choice of what to do if you get the blue screen. It will typically close your software. If it says something about the system being "busy" or "unstable," turn the computer off and back on again.

If you get the blue screen, but by some miracle manage to keep your program open, save your work immediately and reboot.

If you do have to close your software, open it again immediately after rebooting. You may be able to retrieve a version of your work that was rescued by the program.

YOUR COMPUTER FREEZES. Nine times out of 10, a piece of software has tied things into knots.

Hold down the Ctrl and Alt buttons, then tap the Del key. Do this

once. (Doing it more than once will probably cause your computer to reboot.)

You should get a list of everything your machine is running at the moment. If you're lucky, one item will have "Not Responding" listed after its name. That's the problem software. To shut it down, click on it — you should have your mouse back — or use the arrow keys to highlight it. Then click on End Task. You may get a second window telling you "program not responding," and should Windows shut it down? Tell it to go ahead.

If you don't see anything marked as "Not Responding," chances are it's the program you were working on when things went wrong. You can close it, without saving your work, by following the End Task procedure we just talked about. If nothing happens, try it again.

If the program shuts down but your machine is still locked up, hit Ctrl-Alt-Del once to bring up the list of running software again. Now it's time for you to start guessing: Which application has gone awry? Try shutting down other obvious pieces of software first, then graduate to things that look like alphabet soup and are harder to interpret.

Eventually, you'll identify the culprit. Make a mental note of it; chances are, it'll go south again soon.

Don't ever be afraid to shut things down, even the things that aren't immediately identifiable. You won't hurt the computer, though you may prevent it from working correctly again until you reboot, as it searches for the malfunctioning program that you've shut down. ■

Save time with shortcuts

I am about to let you in on a geek secret.

Sometimes, PC tasks that sound really technical and hard are incredibly simple.

Take macros. See? You're ready to quit reading right now. But macros are built into many programs because they're useful, quick and yes, Virginia, easy to use. Simple macros are just a way for you to record your keystrokes and play them back later. Think about this for a second.

There are lots of times when you have to type the same stuff on your computer over and over. When you log in, for example. Or let's say you save Web pages and open them with your word processor. You've got a lot of cleanup to do before they look nice. Do more than one and you realize that you're searching for and replacing the same stuff over and over.

Recording a macro for those tasks would mean you'd only have to do them once. Once you record your keystrokes and mouse clicks, you can just hit a combination of keys or a button on the tool bar and they will play back.

Advanced programmers write their own macros. But you'll never have to bother with that. Whatever you can do with your keyboard and your mouse, you can record to play back later without typing a word of code.

The basic steps for making a macro go like this: Set up the macro, telling the computer what keystrokes or button you want to use to make it run later. Start your recording. Type your keystrokes. Stop recording. That's it.

In Word, Microsoft's powerful word processor, the process looks like this:

Click on Tools, then Macro, then Record Macro. Name your new shortcut and assign it a button or keystroke combination (such as Shift-Ctrl-&). When you hit Assign, then Close, you'll be returned to your document.

A new little window will have music-cassette-style stop and pause buttons. Type, search and replace, use your menus — just do whatever you want recorded. When you're done, click the stop button. You're finished.

That's as hard as it gets. Most software that can have macros works exactly the same way. Check the back of the user's manual under "macro" to see whether your favorite programs include this easy time saver.

You, too, can impress your friends with this incredibly geeky, technical-sounding skill you've learned. You don't have to tell them it was easy. ■

Privacy concerns

f you were surprised at all the hoopla over the ID numbers built into the Pentium III chip, you ain't seen nothing yet.

Just wait until everyone hears about the Microsoft Windows 98 and Office 97 identification features.

Turns out that Microsoft included the ability to identify you and your computer in every copy of Windows 98 and Office 97, a suite of programs that includes Word, Excel and PowerPoint. The ID is also present in Office 98 documents on Apple computers.

The number definitely affects you if you're hooked up to a network or use a cable modem, and it may affect you if you use Internet Explorer or Dial-Up Networking as a connection to the Internet.

Once created, the ID is sent to Microsoft when you register the program and, potentially, sent to every Web site that asks for it — including, to no one's surprise,

www.microsoft.com .

Because the number is sent to Microsoft with the rest of your registration information, this ID is actually more personal than the one people were complaining about in the Pentium III processor chip.

In that case, each chip came with a unique number coded into it. The number could be used to identify a single computer, but not necessarily a name. Privacy advocates registered protests with the Federal Trade Commission in an attempt to block sales of the chip.

But the Windows ID slipped under the radar, generating a fraction of the protests that the Pentium III's code did.

The ID is sent to Microsoft when you register your copy of Windows 98 by using the Registration Wizard that pops up after you install the program, even if you've indicated that you don't want to send any hardware information to Microsoft.

That registration typically includes things like your name and mailing address — information that not only identifies your computer but also identifies you.

The number is stored in the Windows Registry, the master document that tracks everything going on in your system. I don't advise editing the Registry directly unless you're an advanced computer user. And there's no easy way to manually get rid of the Office 97 ID numbers in your documents.

Fortunately for you, Microsoft bowed to public pressure and re-

leased some tools that do the dirty work of disabling the ID. It also eliminated the ID from Windows 98 Second Edition, fixed its Web pages so they no longer request the number and purged the numbers from their marketing databases (not, however, from their tech support files).

This problem does not affect Windows 3.1, 95 or NT users, and it doesn't affect people who have upgraded to Office 2000. Here's how to get software Raid to kill off this pesky bug — er, feature — of Windows 98 and Office 97: Visit **http://officeupdate.microsoft.com/ articles/privacy.htm** and download the Unique Identifier Patch (which prevents future Office documents from carrying an ID) and the Unique Identifier Removal Tool (which scans existing files).

If you haven't upgraded to Service Release 2 of Office 97, the latest version, you'll need to do it before you can install the new software. That's free.

Microsoft has promised that it's going to post a software fix that allows Windows 98 users to eliminate the Windows ID. Unfortunately, that fix hasn't materialized. Your best bet is to update to Windows 98 Second Edition ($20; see the section on the new edition), which eliminates the ID.

If you don't have Web access, call 425-635-7056 for Office technical support, 9 a.m.-9 p.m. weekdays; or 425-635-7222 for Windows 98 support during the same hours. ■

Windows

Windows 98

Microsoft has opened a new Windows for sale.

It has come up with a new version of Windows 98 called Second Edition.

Second Edition looks a lot like the original, which was basically a service upgrade to Windows 95. If you already own Windows 98, you can buy a "Windows 98 Second Edition Updates" CD directly from Microsoft for about $20. It will contain just the latest features.

People who have never used Windows 98 are going to see a few changes. For example, navigating through files on your computer is like using a tiny Web browser window. You can click back to the last folder you were looking at or copy and paste a file by clicking a couple of tool bar buttons.

Some features from Plus!, the add-on CD-ROM for Windows 95, have been built into Windows 98. That includes a scheduler to run programs at preset times and so-called themes for how your desktop looks and sounds. Before, you had to download pieces from the Microsoft Web site or pay around $35 for the Plus! CD.

Some adjustments to the system's guts will please the nerd in you. FAT32, a new way to store files on the hard drive, gets rid of that old 2-gigabyte limit on the size of hard drive letters. (FAT32 was built into later versions of Windows 95.)

The hard drive de-fragmenter program can now store programs used most often in areas that are easiest to get to for the computer. That theoret-ically makes opening programs faster, though I didn't notice much difference.

Windows 98 will also buy you disk space by erasing temporary files. But because many of these would eventually have been erased anyway, this benefit may be limited. If you have more than one monitor and more than one video card, you can use both simultaneously in Windows 98.

It's still more difficult than it needs to be to install and remove hardware and software. Windows 98 will still crash periodically when running programs, and it offers the same incomprehensible explanations for the errors that Win95 did.

Basic functions remain about the same as those in Windows 95, at least as far as what you see on the screen goes. Windows 98 customers have access to Windows Update, which simplifies downloading update files from the Web, as long as you use Microsoft's Internet Explorer as your Web browser.

This is a good time to note that Windows 98 Second Edition comes with both IE5 and NetMeeting 3, Microsoft's latest Web programs. NetMeeting allows you to talk with other Internet users on-line, sharing documents or video feeds if you have the necessary hardware.

If you'd rather use Netscape as your Web browser, go ahead: It works fine under Second Edition, even if you have IE5 installed. I wouldn't rec-ommend uninstalling IE5 on Windows 98 Second Edition, even if you don't use it. Too many IE files are used by other parts of the program.

Second Edition includes the Windows 98 Service Pack, a bunch of upgrades to the core system, including a Y2K update. The Service Pack is also available to current Windows 98 users free at Microsoft's Web site (**www.microsoft.com/windows98**).

Second Edition does include some nice features for high-end users: better home networking support, better lists of automatically supported hardware using Universal Serial Bus (USB) or IEEE 1394 connectors and better support for cable modems.

The most exciting feature for savvy users is likely to be Internet Connection Sharing, which allows all the computers in your house to share a single connection to the Internet. That means you need only one modem or adapter and one phone line. Two or more computers can surf separately on that connection at the same time.

Unfortunately, sharing the connection requires dividing the bandwidth among all the computers you have. So if you're connecting at 28.8 kilobits per second and are sharing the connection between two PCs, each machine is connected at 14.4 kbps.

The home networking and Internet connection sharing capabilities are not for beginners, however They require more computer knowledge and more messing with internal settings than novices might be comfortable with.

If you own Windows 98 and want the Second Edition update, call Microsoft at 800-360-7561. ∎

Microsoft monopolies

I f you see another headline about Microsoft, you're going to scream. I know.

You've heard everything there is to hear about its feud with the U.S. Department of Justice, a slew of state governments and a host of other software companies. The trial's been going on since May 1998, and isn't expected to end until the year 2000. You've heard it all.

Everything, that is, except why you should care.

The bone of contention is Microsoft's Windows 98 operating system and its one controversial twist: including a copy of Microsoft's Explorer Web browser and making it part of the basic structure of the system.

Let's get one thing straight up front: Netscape users can still install and run their program with no problems whatsoever — at least that's been my experience.

So what's the big deal?

Convenience in the software industry has traditionally led to monopoly. That's why this little added convenience for Explorer is a big deal.

Take Windows, for example: It was hardly the best entrant in the operating system market. But because it had a wide distribution network, powered by the marketing savvy in Redmond, Wash., and an established base of DOS users, it was convenient for major software companies to write their programs to run on that system.

Greater choice of programs meant that people who otherwise might

have wavered went straight to Windows. The same thing has happened with Web browsers. More than 50 percent of Web users have now said, why install a new program when Explorer works just fine and comes packaged with my PC?

Take this imaginary scenario:

General Motors suddenly takes over the automotive world, selling the vast majority of new cars. (Yes, I know, Windows isn't on every machine. But it definitely rules the roost.) GM engineers hunt for new convenience features they can add to their new automobiles.

"Ah, I've got it," says one engineer. "Instead of just building in a slot for garage door openers, a feature our customers have really enjoyed, let's actually build the door opener itself into the product. It'll be built-in, so no more problems with rattles or buttons that don't exactly fit our slots."

Suddenly nearly every new car on the market has a built-in remote, which works with one particular type of garage door. People who want to use other garage doors can do so with

no problem. The remote would still rattle around the glove compartment or gets clipped on the sun visor.

But if you were buying a new garage door opener, what brand would you buy? The one with the remote built right into your car? Chances are, unless you were feeling snappish about GM commanding the world's car market, you would.

And that's where the battle started between Microsoft and the government. Building Explorer into Windows 98 does make the Web more convenient, a good thing for customers. But what does that convenience spell for the competition?

Microsoft has made a booming business out of stealing the best features from other programs and incorporating them into its own, as have most successful software makers. If using its near-monopoly on operating system software helps to build a monopoly for its Web browsing software, who will come up with the new features for things that Microsoft can borrow and successfully repackage?

The other thing to consider is: Where will this end? Why shouldn't Microsoft build a copy of its Access database program into a new version of Windows to make it easier for people to store copies of their Rolodexes?

Integrating the entire Office suite into Windows 2001 would be convenient and would certainly make financial sense. But what would it do to the innovative competitors working against Gates' behemoth in those software niches?

That's why you should care. ■

Alternatives to Windows

With Windows' command of the marketplace, it might seem there is no alternative to Microsoft.

But you don't HAVE to use Windows. There are other flavors of operating systems, the basic software that helps your computer run. You've heard of Macintosh, and you may have seen software labeled for Windows NT or OS/2. Each is a good option for some users.

Although none will run the variety of programs that Windows can run, you may find that a different OS crashes less, makes your life easier and even looks better on the screen.

We'll discuss what's out there and where to find information. But first: What is an operating system?

Your computer — the machine — can understand only electrical pulses: on (which it reads as one) or off (zero). For your computer to fulfill your command, the ones and zeros have to line up just right.

Of course, you're not about to start typing in billions of ones and zeros to get your computer to do what you want. That's where the operating system comes in. You talk to the program you're running (like Netscape or Doom). The program talks to your operating system, and your operating system helps translate that request into ones and zeros for your computer.

Your OS also helps make all your programs look and act alike. But new programs and new hardware get invented every day, so your OS has to keep being extended. And that's the downside to an OS. In general, the more programs it can handle, the less stable it becomes. If it doesn't understand what a program is asking, or if it gets some response from your computer's hardware it doesn't know how to handle, or if two programs ask it to do conflicting things, chances are it will crash and take your program with it.

The more stable the operating system, the fewer the errors. But if stability were everything, we'd all still be using DOS and typing in commands rather than clicking on icons. Good operating systems also look nice, are easy to use (or at least predictable) and work well with the software you want to run.

Switching from Windows is a scary prospect. Fortunately, there's a halfway step: You can set up your computer to dual boot, which gives you the option to run either Windows or something else. If Windows is crashing on your favorite game, you can try a different OS. (Windows machines have a version built right in; you can restart your computer in DOS mode.) But if that other OS won't run your checkbook-balancing program, you can revert to Windows.

For how to make your computer do that, check the manual or on-line help for your primary OS or the secondary one you choose.

The major operating systems come in three types: graphic Windows-and-MacOS-like environments, which are relatively easy for mainstream users to try; Unix-style (pronounced you-nix) systems, mostly for techie types; and DOS-like systems, updated versions of the software installed on many early PCs, for the minimalists.

Here's the rundown:

WINDOWS 95/98: Bill Gates made his billions on the backs of Windows 95 and 98. They're familiar, and they will run virtually every software program on the market. They are, however, resource hogs when performing multiple tasks (running more than one program at a time) and are occasionally unstable.

MACOS: If you own an Apple computer, you probably use MacOS. Friendly, informal and fun, it's the beanie to Windows' bowler. It still drags when running multiple programs, and crashes are no fun. There's even less likelihood that you can recover, by stopping the offending program in progress, than in Windows. But it's the OS of choice for desktop publishers, graphic artists and photographers. And many schools still have mostly Macs.

MacOS and Windows used to be so different that they were difficult to compare. Now they've grown similar enough that people can fairly easily move from one OS to the other.

Some companies have stopped making Mac versions of their software because of its sliding market share during the early and mid-1990s. A few picked up production again after Apple's iMac line took off. Still, after Windows products, MacOS has the best selection of software.

WINDOWS NT: Microsoft's more robust version of Windows was originally meant to run on server computers that stored programs and data for lots of other computers hooked up on networks. With the cheap, powerful machines on the market, your next home machine may come with Windows NT installed.

NT is more stable than Windows 95, 98 or MacOS. It's better at recovering from its crashes, and it includes lots of nifty system utilities. But it's built for the business crowd, and although it looks a lot like the Windows home version, it's not always easy to fix and administer. High-end Windows 95/98 games and some non-Microsoft programs won't run well, or at all, on NT.

OS/2: It was hailed by IBM and Microsoft as the Next Big Thing not a decade ago, but then Microsoft bailed out and started hawking Windows, and IBM's attempts to get it accepted in the mass computer market failed.

Yet OS/2 users swear by its grace and stability. On the screen, it looks like the Windows/MacOS group. Its new niche is mostly on major servers, especially in big businesses like banks, where it competes with NT.

OS/2 will run Windows software. It will even run Windows, and some of its users swear it runs Windows better than Windows runs Windows. But IBM has given up on OS/2 upgrades, so it's a dying system.

UNIX SYSTEMS: Unix is a text-based operating system that runs most of the computers hooked up to the Internet. It's great at keeping computers talking to one another. It's extremely stable, and it has a reasonable amount of software — mostly business and computer-to-computer communications related — that will run on it. For the PC, check out these flavors:

Linux: Linux, named after creator Linus Torvalds, has been the only OS recently besides Windows whose market share is growing. The Red Hat version of Linux has spawned a growing number of fans. About five million PC users have some version of Linux now, compared with more than 200 million with Microsoft products, according to International Data Corp. estimates.

Linux takes Unix's stability and adds a graphic screen. It's quick, runs multiple programs well and can play host to such popular programs as Apache, which most computer administrators for the World Wide Web use to host their pages. The downside: It requires great technical skill to plug in the after-market add-ons that really make Linux sing, and software offerings are still limited.

BSDI, FreeBSD, NetBSD, OpenBSD: Different versions of the same program, spawned like the different versions of Linux. Each attempts to bring Unix to the PC. FreeBSD is probably the best supported for home machines. NetBSD and OpenBSD have more networking and business clients. All but BSDI are free, and the source code, like Linux, is available for programmers to tinker with, often right on the program's Web site.

All share some of Unix's great qualities, but are a bit difficult to configure for anyone except experienced PC owners.

MachTen, MacBSD: Like the BSD group, but for Macs.

DOS HYBRIDS: Before Windows, there was DOS: a clunky, text-only operating system that required you to know all the commands to run a program before you even turned the machine on.

As a graduate of a decade of DOS, I'd say thank God for Windows, except that much of Windows' structure is built on old DOS commands. That's why computer geeks seem so smug when they figure out your Windows problems. They're just happy all those years spent working in DOS are worth something!

Despite its drawbacks, DOS was fairly straightforward, had few features and tended to be stable. Some companies are working on DOS clones for folks with old PCs, Windows haters and nostalgic types:

FreeDOS: A free version of DOS (Disk Operating System), which works — most of the time.

DR-DOS: A new version of a really old flavor of DOS (originally called DR-DOS, then changed to OpenDOS, then back to DR-DOS again). Not free, but more stable than Free DOS.

PC DOS: The IBM-brand version. Much like DR-DOS.

For information on Microsoft products, see **www.microsoft.com**.

For alternatives, see **www.altos.org.uk** for links to the companies' home pages, discussion groups and other useful Web sites on those systems. ■

Windows extras

W indows, love it or hate it, is part of most computer users' lives. We get used to its quirks, curse its idiosyncrasies and wait in hope that the next version will be better than this one.

Fortunately, there are a few things you can do to rev up your copy of Windows while you're waiting for the next version.

All of these are available on-line as freeware or shareware. Freeware is totally free software; shareware allows you to download a program free, then asks you to send a contribution if you like it.

WINDOWS 95/98 POWER TOYS: These are advanced tools that the folks at Microsoft developed but don't want to support, so they weren't included in the standard Windows copy.

For the most part, they're

designed for more advanced users. Included are nifty utilities that let you play an audio CD from the task bar, see inside the .CAB folders that Microsoft uses to install files, open Windows Explorer from anywhere, change the resolution of your screen without restarting, open anything on your desktop from the task bar and more.

The best part of the package is definitely TweakUI, which lets you adjust menu speed, mouse sensitivity, some window animation, what your shortcuts look like, which icons are on your desktop and a lot more. This is worth loading even if you skip the rest of the Power Toys.

Find all the Power Toys at **www.microsoft.com/Windows95/ downloads** . (Scroll down until you see the link to the Windows 95 Power Toys Set. Many will also work with Windows 98.)

MTUSPEED: This free utility helps speed up your connection to the Internet by tweaking basic settings in Windows 95. (It won't hurt with Win98, but you might not see the same results.) Check it out at **www.mjs.u-net.com/download. htm** . Be sure to read the "read me" link.

WINDOWS 98 RESOURCE KIT: You get some nifty tools on your Win98 CD that aren't automatically installed when you load the program.

These include ways to compare files and folders, a check for obsolete shortcuts and a few other nifty offerings. To get them, you'll need your Windows 98 CD (it probably came in the box with your PC if you didn't buy it separately), open it, look in the Tools/Reskit directory and run setup.exe. ■

Basic Windows tweaks

WANT A NEW ICON: You can put a picture on the desktop for a shortcut to anything from a letter you're writing to a program you're using.

For a file or program, use the My Computer icon or Windows Explorer. Program names aren't always easy to recognize, so you may have to do some detective work by double-clicking on a file to see whether it's the right one.

When you've got the one you want, click on it with your right mouse button, and a little menu will pop out. Click on the item that says Create Shortcut.

A new icon will appear right in that directory. You can tell that it's not the actual file because it has a so-called swoosh arrow in the lower left-hand corner and says Shortcut. Click on that icon with your mouse, hold down the left mouse button and drag it onto your desktop. You're done.

You can even make an icon for a World Wide Web page you like. Double-clicking on it will start up your Web browser and go straight to that page. To do it in Netscape or Internet Explorer, go to the page and then click your right mouse button anywhere on the screen that does not have a graphic or a link. Pick Create Shortcut (in older versions, it may say Internet Shortcut) and you're done!

I HATE THE TASK BAR: That gray bar at the bottom of the screen always seems to get in the way. But if you set it so that it's not always on top, then you can't get to it when you really need that Start button.

Fortunately, there's a solution. You can set the task bar so that it shrinks to a gray line at the bottom of the screen. When you need it, you just float your mouse cursor over it and it pops right up.

To do it, click on Start, then Settings, then Taskbar. You want to make sure there's a check in the box next to Always on top (so you'll always be able to get to the gray line) and also in Auto hide. That's it — just click OK.

IT'S TOO HARD TO CHANGE MY WALLPAPER: If you want to change the background on your computer screen often, it's just a click away. Put your mouse anywhere on the open desktop (not over an icon!) and click the right button. A little menu will pop out of the screen.

Choose the item that says Properties, and you'll go right to your display settings. Your wallpaper setting should be on the right side. (If not, click on the Background tab to bring that page to the front.)

Pick new wallpaper, click OK and you're done. Another option: If you're surfing the Web and see an image you like, try right-clicking on it and choosing Set as Wallpaper from the menu that pops up. ■

Customizing your Windows icons

Every program you install comes with its own icon, the tiny picture that represents it on your desktop, in its folder on your hard drive or in your Programs menu. Some programs come with a handful of icons. Others ship with dozens.

Icons are handy because you can launch a program by just double-clicking on the little picture. That's why many people like to keep icons of programs they use often out on their desktop.

But after installing a few programs, your computer screen may runneth over with tiny pictures. Fortunately, you can tuck some of them away.

First, you need to understand that both Windows and Apple's MacOS allow you to create duplicates of icons that you can keep in different parts of your computer, on the desktop or hidden away in another sub-menu.

Only one of the icons, though, is the real program. The others are stand-ins for that program. You can delete the stand-ins (shortcuts in Windows, aliases in Macs) without harming the program, but you want to be sure you don't delete the icon that is the program.

Start by looking through the icons on your desktop. You can tell the difference between icons for programs and icons that are shortcuts or aliases by looking in the lower left corner of the little picture. If you see an arrow there (on a PC) or if the text is in italics (on a Mac), that's just a shortcut.

Check your Programs menu (click on Start, Programs) and if you also see icons for the programs there, you can safely delete the ones on your desktop. All icons in the Programs menu are shortcuts, though they don't have the arrow.

If you want the shortcut icons on your desktop but don't want them scattered around, you can create folders on the desktop for storing them. Pick an empty area of the screen and click with your right mouse button. A little menu will pop out; choose New,

then Folder. You'll see the folder appear. Give it a name, then hit the Enter key and it's ready to be used.

You can move icons into that folder from the desktop. Click on an icon and hold down the left mouse button. Now move the mouse, without letting go of the button, to drag the icon on top of the folder. When you see the folder become highlighted, you can let go of the mouse button to drop the icon into the folder. To open a folder to use the icons inside, just double-click on it.

You can get rid of the shortcuts in the Programs menu if you kept those shortcuts on the desktop (or don't need them at all). Do that by clicking on Start, then Settings, then Taskbar. Click on the tab that says Start Menu Programs, then click on the Advanced button. A new window will open.

If you click on the little plus sign next to Programs in this window, you'll see a list of all the folders that you see in your Programs menu. To see what's inside each folder, click on it once. If you see a plus sign next to a folder, it means there are even more folders inside; click on the plus sign to see them.

Now you can start cleaning house. All pictures in these folders are shortcuts, so you can delete them without hurting the program. (If you need to run that software later, and don't have a desktop icon for it, just go to the folder where it's stored, using Windows Explorer or My Computer, and double-click on its icon.)

You can delete a folder or an icon by clicking on it once to select it, then hitting the Delete key on the keyboard. Warning: If you delete a folder, all the icons inside will be erased, too. Be careful! Deleting is a lot easier than adding the icons back later. Make sure you REALLY want to get rid of any shortcuts you delete.

You can add folders to the Program menu if you like. Click once on the word Programs in this window so that it's selected. It will be highlighted. Then click on File, New, Folder. You'll see the new folder appear on the right side of the screen. Give it a name, then hit the Enter key. It's ready to go.

Finally, you can move icons from one folder to another. Click and hold down the left mouse button on the icon you want to move, then drag it over the name of the folder you want it to go into, without letting go of that button. When the name of the folder is highlighted, let go of the button to drop the icon into the folder.

Feeling lonely without all those pictures on your screen? Take a walk down memory lane with Susan Kare, designer of icons for competitors Microsoft Windows (including Solitaire cards, the calculator and Notepad), Apple's MacOS (including the trash can, the Smiley Mac and Clarus, the dogcow who goes Moof!) and IBM's OS/2. Browse her tiny masterpieces at **www.kare.com** . ▪

YOU CAN TELL the difference between icons for programs and icons that are shortcuts or aliases by looking in the lower left corner of the little picture. If you see an arrow there (on a PC) or if the text is in italics (on a Mac), that's just a shortcut.

Other
programs

Microsoft Office

Microsoft is hoping that computer users everywhere want to move into a new Office.

The latest version of its popular suite of business programs is Microsoft Office 2000. It's fatter than ever, with Office Premium typically requiring 525 megabytes of hard drive space and a speedy computer.

It also comes in four versions, which include different combinations of nine programs: Word word-processor, Excel spreadsheet, Outlook e-mail, PowerPoint presentation, Publisher desktop publishing, Access database, FrontPage Web creation, Photodraw business graphics and Small Business Tools.

Here's what you're likely to notice most about Office 2000 compared to Office 97:

BE PREPARED: Got a fast computer and Windows 98? You're in business. But Office 2000 runs slowly on anything with less than 64 megabytes of RAM. If you're running Windows 95, forget it — it's too much work.

Office 2000 replaces so many components of the Windows operating system that a developer who worked on the project joked that this is a mini Windows upgrade, not just a suite of programs.

ONE WARNING: Getting the new Office installed correctly on a newer Windows 95 machine required hours of tech support and obscure commands no one should have to deal with. One benefit of the new Office is supposed to be that it detects when things have gone wrong and fixes itself. That didn't work as advertised here.

CLIP TO YOUR HEART'S CONTENT: One of the welcome changes in 2000 is the ability to cut and paste multiple items at once. Everything you copy or cut is stored in a 12-slot clipboard, and you can choose what you want to paste in from the list.

SAY HELLO TO THE INTERNET: This version of Office does the best job yet of integrating e-mail and the Web into your everyday work. Nearly every part of 2000 has the ability to save your work as a Web page.

Want to send a copy of what you're working on to a single person? Click a button on the tool bar and get an e-mail header on your document inside the program. Fill it out and send it on its way.

CREATE A THEME: Word, FrontPage, Access — several of the Office programs allow you to use themes, common combinations of icons and fonts and backgrounds that make work you did in one program look like the work in another.

CHANGING TOOL BARS: Office doesn't automatically show you all the buttons or all the menu commands available. You can show the complete list at any time by clicking on double chevrons in the tool bars or the menus themselves.

If you figure out where the menu item or button you want lives and use it often, it will automatically add itself to the main tool bar or menus.

LITTLE SURPRISES: The worst surprise is that multiple documents in programs such as Word now open in multiple windows, so clicking on the X-to-close box in the upper right corner doesn't close the program; you'll end up hitting it multiple times. (Choosing File, then Exit still works.)

The best surprise may be the drop-down list for fonts, which lets you choose from all the typefaces — as they would display on the screen.

Saving files to places other than the default My Documents folder is much easier in 2000; large icons guide you to commonly used places or the Desktop. ■

PalmPilot programs

If you've gotten 1999's trendiest gift, 3Com's hugely popular PalmPilot organizer — whether's it's a Palm IIIx, Palm 5 or even a Palm VII — it's time to get moving. Learn how to make it more productive, and it won't gather dust at the bottom of your desk drawer.

To get you started, here's a list of some cool software you can use with your Palm. (Wait! I see you folks who don't own or care about PalmPilots leaving the room. Ever wonder what makes your geeky friends want to carry them around? This list might tell you.)

These programs all share two important characteristics: They're tiny, so they won't take up much of your Pilot's precious memory. And they're free, or nearly free, because I'm a cheapskate. No, not really. It's because most Pilot software is inexpensive. Any program here not otherwise marked is free. (Reason No. 1 to love your Pilot.)

BOOKS: The next time you're waiting in the doctor's office, catch up on the classics. Hundreds of books for the Pilot are available free on-line, and you can add them to your PalmIII one chapter at a time and browse through them using AportisDoc Reader.

BUSINESS: If you want to carry around spreadsheets, databases or other work tools, the Pilot has software that will read and convert standard types and allow you to synchronize with work on your desktop PC. Pilot MiniCalc synchronizes with Excel for $15. MobileDB Lite lets you read databases. MobileDB lets you edit databases for $15.

CALCULATORS: Your Pilot can do everything from figuring out how much you should tip (TipCalc) to calculating how much your car payment would be on a particular deal. (FCPlus, at $20, is a particularly nice package.)

GAMES: You did not buy or receive this incredibly useful device just so you could play games on it, as if it were any common GameBoy. But now that you've got it ...

If you're a fan of shoot-'em-ups, role playing or especially interactive text adventures, the Pilot has a slew. I admit that one of my big thrills this holiday season was discovering that a free converter named Pilot-Frotz allows me to play old Infocom games, such as the Zork series, on the PalmIII.

THE NET: Did you know that your Pilot can read e-mail (using programs such as TopGun Postman or Multimail Discovery, which costs $10) and surf the Web (using ProxiWeb) on your existing Internet account? If you're into sending instant messages to folks, you can even use ICQ for the Pilot. These functions require the PalmPilot modem, which runs about $100.

Finally, a little program called AvantGo will download Web sites from your Internet account when you link your Pilot and your PC, so you can read those pages while you're out wandering.

TRAVEL: Want to figure out currency conversions on the fly, track your frequent flier miles or learn a few phrases in a new language? More programs than I can list here will do each one for you. Search on PalmGear H.Q. for the Travel category.

HandMap even lets you browse electronic maps of selected states and areas, including Michigan. The program is free; you pay $6-$16 for each county map.

WHERE TO GET THEM:

My favorite Palm site on the Web is PalmGear H.Q., at **www.palmgear.com** .

Just about all these programs can be found there. For ICQ, check out **www.icq.com** .

For TipCalc, see CNet's excellent Pilot downloads site at **www.download.com** . (Click on the Downloads for PalmPilots link.)

And for FCPlus, see **www.infinitysw.com** . ▄

Fax programs

One of the nice things about having a computer at home is the ability to send and receive faxes when you need them. Most modems come with faxing software. Check the guide that came with your computer to find out where it is in your Programs menu.

If you have a separate phone line for your computer, you can set your PC to answer the phone as a fax machine whenever it's on. Otherwise, you'll have to manually start the fax program and tell it to answer the phone when you're expecting a fax call.

Once you've received the fax, you'll see it on the screen. You can now print what you see, or save it to your hard disk to look at later. Full-featured fax programs include optical character recognition (OCR) software, which attempts to translate the fax image into text you can edit. But be warned: The technology is hardly perfect. If the letters are at all garbled on the fax, expect to correct a lot of typos.

Sending is even easier. When you install your fax software (if it wasn't already installed when you bought the computer), it probably created a ghost printer where your computer can send files. If you want to fax a document, click on File, then Print from inside the program where you created the document.

When you get the usual dialogue box asking you how many pages and which pages you want to print, click on the down arrow (the little gray box with the downward-pointing black triangle) next to your printer's name. You'll see all the other printers your system is set up to use. If you're working at home, you'll probably see only your actual printer and one other name: the fax program in your machine.

Click on the name of the fax program and click on the Print button. Now your fax program will open automatically, allowing you to fill in the number where you want to send your document, cover page information and any other options it provides. ■

Controlling your PC remotely

You're at home and you desperately need that file from work. Or you're at work and you desperately need that noodle recipe from your home computer.

What to do? Well, if both those computers have a modem connected to a phone line, it's time to start thinking about remote access software.

Back in the dark ages of the early '80s, remote access software was used by thousands of computer owners to dial in to other machines to chat. It also let users call central machines called Bulletin Board Systems (BBSs), where they could read and send messages, files and mail to other people who dialed into that same BBS.

The screen was ugly, the commands were clunky, and all you saw was text. Controlling the other person's PC required semi-legal hacking skills, and the person on the other end was never really free from the danger of computer pirates.

Like everything else in the PC world, remote access software has made some dramatic changes. Now you can dial into your computer at work or at home and control it just as if you are there.

You see the screen on the other computer, control it with your mouse and keyboard, and have access to everything stored on your hard drive. Security features in the new software help protect your machine, so only you can do the controlling.

You can set passwords to protect your other PC from folks who figure out what number to dial, and you can also tell it not to accept calls for longer than a second or two. Instead, when it's contacted, it will call back a number you set earlier. That way, you dial in from your other PC and it calls you back.

Remote access software also helps the person with a laptop and a desktop PC. It can make sure that your files are up to date on both machines and that access from the road is a breeze.

New-generation remote access software also speeds up file transfers between your two PCs by compressing them before sending or just sending the part of the file you changed. Some let you download a so-called plug-in to a Web browser, allowing you to control your PC from any Web-able machine you can find.

If you want your computers to talk while you're asleep — to make sure certain files are the same in both places, say, despite the day's changes — many programs can schedule that in the middle of the night.

And the programs allow you to chat on-screen to anyone who happens to be using your computer at the time.

Some programs to try:

PCANYWHERE (Symantec, 800-441-7234, **www.symantec.com/pcanywhere**, $149 list) claims to be the market leader in remote access. It has most of the bells and whistles we've discussed, plus a few that help make life easier. It automatically reduces the number of colors transmitted to your screen to speed up your connection. It will also scan files for viruses before you transmit or accept them.

COSESSION REMOTE 32 V8 (Artisoft, 800-846-9726, **www.artisoft.com**, click on Products then CoSession, $119) does all the basics and includes user profiles, so you can give differing access to your machine depending on who is dialing in.

CARBON COPY (Compaq, 800-888-9909, **www.carboncopy.com**, $99) will allow you to connect to your PC over the Internet, reducing those long-distance calls. It also has a nice scheduler for doing tasks later.

LAPLINK (Traveling Software Inc., 800-343-8080, **www.laplink.com**, $149; or $49 for Remote DeskLink, which offers more limited functions) keeps your laptop and desktop PCs talking. It has great file synching utilities and will pick up a file transfer in progress later if you get cut off. ■

Tax & personal finance software

I n January, computer users' hearts lightly turn to thoughts of ... taxes.

Yes, those W2s and 1099s start rolling in, and the thought of having to wade through all those forms makes your blood pressure rise. Fortunately, two excellent programs can help.

Intuit's TurboTax Deluxe ($45; **www.turbotax.com**) and Kiplinger's TaxCut Deluxe ($35; **www.taxcut .com**) software are top-selling choices, and they both do a good job of completing your return. Either one will walk you through the wages, mortgage interest, capital gains and home-business expenses many filers deal with. They're aimed squarely at the home computer user, so don't expect beefy business return options.

My nod for 1999 goes to TaxCut — barely. (See my column on the Web at **www.freep.com/tech/pcathome** for a year 2000 update.) It's smarter about showing you information about your taxes based on the answers you give to questions. But TurboTax, with its professional design and excellent tax-planning features, is hot on its heels.

First, a warning: Both programs work best if you have Internet access. That's because you can download updates until the deadline arrives, and, in the case of TaxCut, download software for your state return free. Updates are important not only because the IRS often leaves crucial decisions about taxes until the end of the year but also because glitches in the programs themselves are often fixed in later versions.

Both programs provide a free way to electronically file your taxes, a process that can speed returns and eliminate IRS data-entry mistakes. Both are available now in most computer stores.

And now for the major differences:

THE SCREENS: TurboTax wins the presentation battle hands down. Its videos are more professional, and it rarely requires you to mess with the actual forms unless you choose to enter your information that way. TaxCut makes it easier to identify entries as tentative, which is helpful if you're preparing a return with missing paperwork.

THE HELP: Both TurboTax and TaxCut have excellent help menus and IRS publications available at the click of a mouse. TaxCut's instructions are a bit clearer. Both include tax manuals from respected publishers.

THE TECHNICAL: TurboTax will import your Quicken financial data seamlessly into your returns. TaxCut will use either Quicken or Money, but requires you to go through several steps to convert the files. TaxCut had trouble finding the computer's Internet connection to download updates automatically; TurboTax had no problems. But TaxCut was quicker to spot earlier installations of software — including, ironically, TurboTax — and suggest bringing in data from there.

THE RETURN: Both do a fine job of filling out the necessary forms on a sample return. TaxCut was smart enough to guess that a journalist might have freelance expenses and to suggest that small-business forms might be in order. TurboTax helps figure out exactly what contributions could be made to a retirement plan from that self-employment income, but doesn't calculate what the person might be able to contribute into a regular deductible IRA.

TaxCut suggests the regular IRA deduction, but doesn't provide a worksheet to calculate the business retirement plan. This is a fairly typical example of the differences between the two programs: mostly a matter of bells and whistles that one includes and the other doesn't.

THE EXTRAS: TurboTax provides a great planning worksheet that instantly shows the results of increasing your deductions next year or decreasing your income. But TaxCut lets you prepare this year's state income tax returns free (or for $5.95 for a CD with all states if you don't have Internet access). With TurboTax, you have to buy each state's forms separately.

FILING ON-LINE: Both Intuit and Kiplinger offer secure Web filing of returns without requiring you to buy their software. TaxCut limits you to the 1040EZ return at **www.taxcut.com**, but that's free. TurboTax has its full program on-line at **www.webturbotax.com**, but it'll cost you $10-$20 to prepare your return unless you're a client at a handful of financial institutions or have an annual income of less than $20,000.

Both sites use advanced encryption technology, so the chances are excellent that the only people to see your return will be the folks at the electronic filing center and IRS staff.

A NOTE: Apple users, the MacOS version of TurboTax is called MacInTax. Both programs are available for Apple computers. ■

Games

Zork

I wonder sometimes what it was like to grow up without television. Or without radio. What a show-stopper those first programs must have been! Who would have cared what was on? It was the box itself that caused the stir.

I felt the same way when we first brought a PC into my house in 1980. I had used a mainframe system at school for a year before we brought the first one home, but the excitement was big when we turned that machine on.

I remembered that feeling recently as I started to play "Zork Grand Inquisitor." It's adventure game software based on a series of titles first created at the Massachusetts Institute of Technology in the late '70s by students who wanted to play games over the school's computer network.

I can't describe the wonder I felt the first time I plugged in one of those old, giant floppy disks (remember when they really were floppy?) and ran the first "Zork" game. There were no graphics, of course, and no sound. You used typed sentences to tell the game what you wanted to do — "Light lamp," or "Give the bread to the old man" — and it responded by describing the results.

I know: Compared with "Myst," this sounds like Dullsville. Not only that, but it was hard. My husband and I solved "Myst" in a weekend. There's no way I could approach that with "Zork."

Still, it was so amazing to watch the computer respond differently depending on what you typed in. That's the way I felt about everything related to computers then: It was amazing just to watch it happen.

I can remember being in a Zen-like state as I waited to dial in to the local computer bulletin board with my 300-bits-per-second modem. It would take half an hour to get in because there was just one phone line. So I'd set my modem to try over and over again. I was unable to leave the room because I'd get hung up on if I finally got in and didn't type anything immediately. The wait didn't end once you logged in, of course. I can still read faster than a 300-baud modem realistically transmits.

It seems foolish now, in the days when a single busy signal from my Internet provider drives me batty. But it was such a thrill to talk to the community of other computer users there — a retired postman, a computer store owner, a bunch of high school students scattered over the city and all the others — that it was worth the wait.

Times have changed. I avoid Internet newsgroups because of the time they take. Even flashy graphics, great soundtracks and brand-name actors can't addict me to the new computer games. I'm frustrated if my computer slows for any reason, and I find myself flipping it on to perform a task, then turning it back off.

I've gone from taking country drives with my computer and admiring the scenery to just commuting with it.

Still, every once in a while, I'm reminded of that original sense of wonder. I can't describe my childlike joy when the new "Zork Grand Inquisitor" game, with all its modern frills, picked up characters and conventions from the first text versions. I was delighted to discover that if I wandered in dark places, I'd be eaten by a grue. Or that I'd have to visit a white house with a mailbox to get where I needed to go.

It was like being able to step back into my shoes of 20 years ago and re-experience that sense of awe.

I'm going to try to hang on to that feeling. People new to home computers, disappointed because the machines are unreliable and occasionally difficult, tell me they wonder how we computer pioneers had the patience to learn to deal with these things.

I usually tell them I don't know. But now I'm going to remember the rapt look I must have worn while I looked at the flickering screen — so like the youngsters who watched the first TV or listened to the first radio.

You can still buy the old "Zork" text adventures as part of the Infocom Masterpieces collection for $16.95. Visit Activision's Web site, **http://store.activision.com**, then click on PC in the left column. It's also available at some retail computer stores. You can even download some of them from various fan sites on the Internet. Search for "Zork I" to find a few. ■

Riven

Myst lovers spent four years preparing themselves for the sequel to the popular computer game. But once Riven arrived, many of their PCs were not ready.

Riven offers the same crisp three-dimensional worlds, haunting music and endless gadgets that Myst featured. There's another engrossing trip through fantastic scenery and fabulous story lines. The trick for many people when it was released, however, was running it.

Riven required a Pentium 100 PC with 16 megabytes of RAM, 75 megabytes of hard drive space, a 4X CD-ROM, a video card capable of displaying 640x480 screen resolution with millions of colors and, of course, Windows 95.

The Mac version required a 90Mhz PowerPC, System 7.5, 9 MB RAM, 65 MB hard disk space and a 4X CD-ROM.

It's true that these specifications weren't outlandish for a high-end game and that you could buy a PC with these qualities for $1,000 then. (Chances are, your computer now will run it with ease.) But many of the people who made Myst a best-seller complained that they didn't have the machines to run the sequel.

If this were a program aimed at the high-end set, I'd have dismissed any concerns about its requirements. Manufacturers have discovered that young men, the primary game audience, are willing to shell out the bucks for a top-of-the-line system to get the best performance.

But Riven was designed to attract the same folks as Myst. And Myst was different.

Myst was remarkable not only for its dazzling graphics but also for its mass appeal. It sold 3.5 million copies.

It didn't sell to just the traditional computer game audience, either. Part of its success was that virtually anyone with a CD-ROM drive could play.

That's definitely not the case with Riven, and that has robbed millions of advancing the Myst experience they really enjoyed — all of which is too bad, because I loved playing Riven. It's a worthy successor to Myst.

Like the first game, it doesn't ask you to shoot anyone, play cards or test your reflexes. You are sent to new worlds to help rescue Catherine, the wife of Atrus (the guy from the end of Myst). If you don't know who these people are, don't worry; you don't have to have played Myst to enjoy Riven.

You can walk around the landscape, touch things, move stuff and generally feel as if you're actually there.

Like Myst, Riven should take a minimum of a weekend of solid play to solve, and most people will probably work at it off and on for months. Riven is every bit as beautiful, captivating and puzzling as Myst. That's what makes it such a shame that everyone who loved the first game didn't get to play the second.

We asked newspaper readers to tell us what they thought of Myst.

HERE'S A SAMPLING:

"My grandson got Myst for Christmas, and he and I started playing it together in Michigan and him in North Carolina. It was so much fun to have an interest together, especially since he is 10 and I am 65. He thinks Grandma is pretty computer-savvy."
— **Joy Johnson, retired nurse, Hudsonville, Mich.**

"Myst was not only my first purchase after acquiring a CD-ROM drive; it was a primary reason for buying (the drive) in the first place. Each puzzle's logic made sense to me, and the multiple-destination design allowed my 'lumpy thinking' to mull over several puzzles at once."
— **John M. Hebert, library clerk and retired U.S. Army logistician, New Baltimore, Mich.**

"When I first heard and viewed Myst on my monitor, I was enthralled. The graphics and music within Myst are lovely, and the puzzles are not solved easily. So I definitely have never been bored with it; it's still a challenge and a thing of beauty."
— **Barb Kapplinger, volunteer, Farwell, Mich.**

"I thoroughly enjoyed the game ... even though I died twice trying to solve the whodunit."
— **Rob Brousseau, software trainer, Ann Arbor, Mich.**

Internet

Getting
started

Free Internet access & e-mail

If you want to start using e-mail but you're worried about the expense, there are plenty of ways to get an account free (or nearly free).

Juno, probably the best-known free e-mail provider, has been in business for a couple of years. It will give you the software and the dial-up number to get into your account. In exchange, you're exposed to advertising from Juno sponsors.

Call 1-800-654-5866 for information, or if you can, check out **www.juno.com** .

You'll be charged $9 if you need disks mailed to you.

Juno runs on a 386 or better with Windows 3.1 and up. No DOS or Apple versions are planned.

More than a dozen companies will give you free e-mail access if you can get to a machine that can view the World Wide Web.

Two of the most popular are HotMail, at **www.hotmail.com** , and Yahoo! Mail, at **http://mail .yahoo.com** .

Again, you're going to be looking at the ever-present ads, but they're no more annoying than the banners you see on most Web pages these days.

For a list of some other free e-mail services, check out **www.geocities .com/CollegePark/Quad/6680 /email.htm** or **http://members.aol .com/IXL2000/page9.html** for two Web pages put together by enthusiasts.

Many sites will give you free Web storage, though not free

Web access. Try hosting your pages at **www.webjump.com** or **www.geocities.com** .

If you need more than e-mail but still have a tight budget, consider some cheap local resources. Many libraries are members of the Library Network, which offers cheap Internet access to everyone.

Some local Internet providers offer inexpensive scaled-down plans ($9 and up) if you think you'll be using the Net only for a few hours each month. Check the Yellow Pages under "Internet" and you'll find a list.

Call your long-distance company and find out whether you can get a deal. Most will offer you a year of free Internet service (limited to just a few hours of use a month) if you're a cus-

tomer. After that, you'll pay monthly fees.

You also might consider taking a college course. Most community and four-year colleges offer free or discounted Internet service to their students, and registering for a single one-credit course often makes you eligible. For short-term use, consider America Online or CompuServe. Both offer 30-day free trials. If you haven't already gotten one of their free disks in the mail, check out computer magazines. At least one will be plastic-wrapped with an AOL disk inside.

In the Detroit area, there's another option: the Greater Detroit Free-Net.

This free, dial-in service is run by a nonprofit corporation. It gives anyone in the area with a computer and modem free e-mail, as well as text access to government and other information. There are more than two dozen dial-in numbers scattered across the southeastern quarter of the state.

For more information, call 1-313-226-9466 or send a self-addressed, stamped envelope to: Greater Detroit Free-Net, 1212 Griswold, 9th Floor, Detroit 48226-1899.

Cities across the country have or are planning similar services, so contact your local public library to learn whether there's one forming close to you.

Finally, don't forget to ask your employer whether e-mail access is available for workers. ■

Choosing an Internet provider

Marcel Halberstadt opened his phone bill and stared at it in shock. It was $455, more than four times his usual amount. He scanned the list of toll calls and immediately saw the problem: The local dial-up number his Internet provider had given him was not so local after all.

It would take the air quality consultant from Farmington Hills, Mich., weeks to get the problem resolved.

He got a complete list from the phone company of all exchanges that were, in fact, local calls from his home. He slogged through on-line directories of Internet providers and called company after company, discarding those that had gone out of business, didn't service local customers or didn't follow through on promises to send out start-up kits or promotional information.

One of the companies that had promised to send him information and have a representative call back to hook him up never called or wrote to him again. That didn't stop it from billing him, however.

"I've been getting monthly invoices for a service they have never provided," he said. "I have been treated very cordially by them each time I've called and reminded them that they're billing me in error, but I do hope the invoices will finally stop coming."

Finally, he found a provider that offered truly local service and signed up. He was then surprised to find that his original provider did indeed have a local number for him — in a different area code.

Just as the number in his area code had been long distance (despite not requiring him to dial a 1), this number was local, even though he was required to dial 1 and the area code. So he kept that account for his business and now has two service providers.

"I've learned a few lessons in going through this exercise," he said. "Perhaps the most frustrating was that no one could tell me whether their access number in my general vicinity would be a local call for me."

It's not easy these days to find the right connection to the Internet. Ameritech lists 481 Internet service providers (ISPs) in its Michigan yellow pages, and those are just companies that paid for ads. The List (**www.thelist.com**), a national directory, lists 7,200 companies and is still not complete.

Those companies are fighting to get their share of the billions Americans spend on Internet service each year. In 1998, we paid nearly $8 billion; International Data Corp. estimates that in a few years, ISPs could bring in 10 times that much.

Bruce Kasrel, a senior analyst at Forrester Research, thinks that estimate is a little high, but agrees that spending will double or triple over the next few years as the number of people on-line increases.

The gorilla is America Online, which controls 42 percent of on-line subscriptions in the United States and attracts a majority of new Internet users. But the rest of the jungle is up for grabs. In fact, equal percentages of subscribers are split among tiny providers that control less than 2 percent of the market each.

Forrester Research analysis shows that customers are pretty much the same regardless of which ISP they use. That means that everybody's fighting for the same people: people like you.

Although all this competition makes it difficult to pick one company, it's also bringing down prices. Unlimited accounts are as cheap as $9.95 a month nearly everywhere, thanks to the glut of ISPs.

"We all dream that we're going to add services that people will be willing to pay more for," said Duane Rao, chief executive of BigNet Holdings in Sterling Heights, Mich., whose Internet branch provides dial-up service to 20,000 Michiganders. "But I believe prices are going to stay right where they are for a few years."

BigNet has been pouring ever-increasing amounts of money into radio, print and television ads in an attempt to set itself apart from its growing competition. It has spent an estimated $750,000 this year, three times as much as 1998.

Still, you'll find a lot more providers in the phone book than you will on TV.

If you have Net access now at home, at work or through your local library, visit two large directories: The List (address above) and BoardWatch, at **www.boardwatch**

.com . (Click on ISP Directory, then Find an ISP). Both allow you to search by area code.

Once you've got a list of providers near you, you'll need to answer these questions:

DO YOU NEED UNLIMITED ACCESS?

Most providers offer plans that allow you to connect for as many hours a day as you like. Others offer limited-hour plans for which you pay a premium for time spent over your limit.

Don't underestimate how much time you plan to spend on-line. As more opportunities to buy and discuss and learn go up on the Web, Americans are spending more time on the Net.

Media Metrix Inc. estimated in May 1999 that the average person spends about eight hours a month on-line. That's not bad, considering that the number includes people who visit only occasionally. And those hours were up about 45 percent from the previous year.

IS THERE A DISCOUNT FOR PAY-ING IN ADVANCE?

To get that $9.95 BigNet rate, you've got to pay for two years up-front. Rao says 80 percent of his customers do. Many companies now offer discount prices for users who pay six months or a year ahead. Those low prices can be appealing, but they prevent you from switching after a month or two if you get bad service.

Another prepayment concern, experts said, is the stability and longevity of the company. You could pay for two years' service, only to see the provider go under six months

later. Make sure your company has an established track record.

IS IT A LOCAL CALL TO DIAL IN?

Unless you're buying a specialized system, such as a cable modem or satellite service, you're probably going to be using your phone line to dial into the provider's computers. You don't want to be paying long-distance charges for that call if you can avoid it.

"With all of the competition, one should always be able to find an ISP that will have a local access number. Being on the Internet seems to go by much faster than talking on the phone, and paying long distance can get expensive in a hurry on your computer," said John R. Kelley, a foreign language instructor in the Chippewa Valley (Mich.) School District.

Be sure to check the local access number to make sure it's really local, not just in the same area code.

"I made this mistake once," said Terry Bone, technical specialist for Ford Motor Credit Co. "Picking an ISP that has a local access number in your area will save you having to call the phone company to try to explain away all those

huge charges."

If you're frequently on the road, you might want a national company that can provide local access numbers around the country or around the globe. Most providers have a directory of the cities or area codes where they have local access.

"For me, a big issue is the ability to connect from just about anywhere in the U.S.," said John E. Levis, a Livonia, Mich., research consultant. "I travel fairly often, and having a local dial-up number is important. My provider also has an 800 number."

IS THE NUMBER BUSY?

"I think the No. 1 ISP user complaint is frequent busy signals," said Dick Minnick, senior technical specialist at Ford Systems Integration Center.

If you can, talk the provider into giving you the local access number for your area BEFORE you sign up. Then dial that number with your regular phone periodically. If you hear a computer screeching, you're in business. One busy signal is bad news; two in a day should cause you to look elsewhere.

A provider with too many customers for its hardware will also force you to wait longer for pages to load, a problem called latency.

"You can ask when you call, but they aren't going to tell you if they're oversubscribed," said Harold Willison, senior network engineer at Apex Global Internet Services.

He suggests checking out how good a connection the provider has to the so-called Internet backbone, the main pipes that transmit information around the country.

The BoardWatch directory lists that number under Total Bandwidth for each provider, measured in kilobits (thousands of bits) or megabits (millions of bits) per second. That speed is split between all the users on-line at a given time, so the bigger the better.

IS THE PROVIDER COMPATIBLE WITH YOUR MODEM?

Most providers now support the "v.90" protocol, which allows different brands of 56 kilobit-per-second modems to talk to one another. Make sure that your chosen company does and that your modem does as well. Otherwise, you'll need to find a provider that supports your particular 56kbps type: either K56flex or x2.

You should make sure that your local dial-in number is ready for 56K speeds, too. Some providers haven't upgraded all their modems yet.

CAN YOU GET TECH SUPPORT?

Make sure the hours for tech support match the hours you plan to use the service. It's not much help to have stellar support during business hours if you're using your account mostly on the weekends.

You might also try calling the tech support number before signing up for service to make sure you don't get a busy signal or a request to hold for extended periods of time.

"I may not be typical, but I am afraid to attempt any changes with my Internet connection," said Jack Kircher, a physician's assistant who works for the state of Michigan. "For me, a simple change gone wrong means hours trying to fix it. Available technical support is number one on my list of qualities to look for in a new ISP."

WHAT SERVICES DO YOU NEED?

Some providers offer multiple e-mail addresses as part of one account, which is helpful for families.

Some offer Web hosting, good for your small business. Make sure yours allows access to newsgroup discussion groups or chat channels, if you're interested in participating. Are those groups censored?

One useful feature is the ability to pick up your mail from a Web site. That way, if you're out of town, you can still check your e-mail without having to tweak the settings on someone else's Internet account.

On the flip side, if you can live with very basic services, you can reduce your bills by buying a limited account. Anthony M. Camilletti Sr. of Clinton Township, Mich., is happy with his Juno Gold account, which provides him with e-mail but no Web access.

"The service suits me beautifully and only costs $2.95 a month," he said. "One consideration is fear: I'm afraid the Internet will take over my very being. I have many friends who tell me that isn't true, yet I can hardly get them on the phone because they're on the Internet virtually all day.

"My wife and I have been married 48 years, and I feel that this is not the time for me to let anything interfere with our lives together."

HOW MUCH STORAGE DO YOU WANT?

Most accounts have a limit on how much space you can take up with your e-mail. If it's too small an amount, you may come back from vacation to find your mailbox full and your incoming messages bouncing back to their senders, said Marcie V. Smith, owner of One Stop Internet. She recommends 5 megabytes minimum.

You may also get free Web page storage space with your account. The more you have, the more pictures and sounds you can include with your

site. Also keep an eye on how much traffic you're allowed. If there's too much, you could be hit with some stiff fees.

Finally, find out whether your provider allows you to use your personal Web space to post business pages and whether it will allow you to host a domain name (one of those unique Web names, such as **www.freep.com**).

DO YOU NEED SPECIAL KIDS' SERVICES?

A few providers offer filtering of Web pages, incoming mail and other information for offensive material.

WHAT DO YOU GET FREE?

Some providers ship a suite of free software to use while surfing. Others offer money-back guarantees that you'll be satisfied.

DO OTHER USERS LIKE IT?

"Word of mouth is a great reference for selecting an ISP," said Mike Bader of LAN Solutions in Utica, Mich. "Try to find someone that will use the system like you do. If you're a heavy user, a person that just checks their e-mail once a day isn't the best reference.

"Find someone that has used the service for a while or maybe tried a few, to compare experiences." ■

Problems with your connection

The Internet offers incredible services to people in rural areas. Everything from medical information to shopping is available — without the grueling drive to a larger city.

So it's too bad that many rural residents will never get a chance to use the Net.

First, folks outside cities rarely have a computer store nearby. They have to rely on mail-order and long-distance calls to technical support.

Next, they usually do not have a local number to dial into if they want access to America Online, CompuServe or the Internet. Even people in suburban cities may have a struggle finding a local number. In rural areas, getting high-speed communication through a digital ISDN line or cable modem is an electronic dream.

Finally, thanks to their phone lines, some rural residents may never be able to communicate via PC at all.

Take Carole Charney, who lives in Leonard, at the northern end of Oakland County, Mich. As a registered nurse, she hoped to continue her education using the Net. As the mother of a seventh-grader, she was hoping to help her son do homework and avoid long road trips to the library.

"Everything's about 20 to 30 minutes away for us here," she said.

But Charney and a neighbor had been having no end of trouble getting on-line and were finally told by the phone company that their location meant they would probably never be able to use their modems successfully.

The phone company, Ameritech, isn't the bad guy in this case. It refunded a good chunk of the money Charney spent on a second line, was up-front about the problem once it was diagnosed and complied with all federal telephone line quality rules.

Ameritech's Bill McSorley of Detroit explained the problem: Every telephone wire makes a loop from the customer's house to the nearest telephone company switch. As this loop gets longer, McSorley said, "you can't get as much performance."

The line gradually stops transmitting higher frequencies, which we don't use much for talking on the phone, but which sophisticated modems require.

The speed the modem can transmit drops as the line gets longer until — in cases like Charney's — the modem can't communicate effectively at all.

There are two solutions to the problem, both expensive: Replace the wires from the switch to the house with more capacity or upgrade the equipment on the line to get stronger transmission.

Less than 5 percent of Ameritech's clients suffer from Charney's problems. But it is precisely this 5 percent that needs those lines the most. These people can't get home Internet access any other way.

There's no easy solution. Even broadcast-based options such as WebTV use a phone line for some functions. For people who need to use their PCs, the unfortunate reality is that rural areas are always last on everyone's list. They're too unprofitable to consider important.

It's up to us to tell our representatives and our government that electronic communication is vital for everyone, not just those living in big cities. Telephone line standards should reflect the new ways people share information, especially for those who need it most. ■

Your computer's Net performance

You love the Internet. You hate the wait. What to do?

You can cut the time it takes to see a new Web page or download a file with these tricks.

BUY A NEW MODEM. Your computer's processing speed doesn't slow down your Net connection nearly as much as a slow modem, and with prices at rock bottom — a brand-name 3Com 56-kilobits-per-second model is selling by mail order for $50 and up — you have no reason to hang on to a slow one.

SWITCH INTERNET PROVIDERS. If your provider doesn't yet support 56kbps, find one that does. And if you couldn't find a provider that offered a local phone number to dial the last time you checked, ask about that, too. The number of lines that each company offers is increasing rapidly. Check the Yellow Pages under "Internet."

GET IN SYNC WITH YOUR PROVIDER. In the early days of 56kbps modems, there were two competing technologies, led by 3Com/U.S. Robotics and Lucent Technologies. Both could communicate at 56kbps, but only with another modem using the same technology. An international group later standardized rules for 56kbps transmissions, making it possible for 3Com- and Lucent-style modems to talk to each other. But some providers have been slow to upgrade.

If you're buying a new modem, call your Internet service company. If the provider uses the new standard, called v.90, you can buy nearly any new modem available. (Just make sure that it hasn't been sitting on the shelf forever, so that it, too, supports the v.90 protocol).

If the provider doesn't use v.90, find out what kind of modems it uses and buy the same style. (3Com-style modems use "x2" technology; Lucent-style use "K56flex.")

Finally, if you already have a 56kbps modem that is not compatible with your provider's type but your provider is upgrading to v.90, find out from your modem manufacturer whether you can upgrade your existing modem to get on the v.90 bandwagon. Most are offering free software to make the switch.

MAXIMIZE YOUR MTU. This is a bit esoteric, but it can definitely affect the download speeds of Windows users, especially if you use Windows 95. Here's a great analogy from NetPro Northwest, one of the Web sites discussing this problem (**www.infinisource.com /maxmtu.htm**):

Picture sending a letter over the Net. Your computer neatly cuts that piece of paper into smaller pieces called packets. Each packet is separately labeled with the destination before it's sent out. How big each piece of paper is when it leaves is set by something called the MTU, or Maximum Transmission Unit, in Windows. The smaller the MTU, the smaller the pieces of paper.

The standard paper size for Windows 95 is 1,500 bytes. But many Internet computers are set to handle much smaller packets of 576 bytes. When they get oversized packets, they have to cut them into smaller pieces, readdress the new pieces and send them on their way. This can delay your transmission times by up to 50 percent.

Lowering the MTU value of the transmissions you send out, to make the packets flow smoothly through the Net, requires fiddling with the Windows Registry, which is not recommended for any but the most advanced computer users. Fortunately, several companies have packaged the changes into easy-to-use software.

One great, free version called MTUSpeed is available for downloading off the Net. Point your browser to: **www.mjs.u-net.com /download.htm** .

When you see software packages that promise to increase your Internet speed by up to 100 percent, you're looking at an MTU-fixing program. I tried one, called CheckIt NetOptimizer, to see whether I got any better performance than I did after using MTUSpeed. I didn't, and the utilities that come with NetOptimizer, while handy, take 10 megabytes of hard drive space. (Total size of MTUSpeed: 400 kilobytes, or about one-twentieth the space.)

NONE OF THESE CHANGES

will affect you if you're not using a telephone to connect to the Net — for instance if you have a cable modem, ISDN line or ADSL service. (The MTU fix also does not affect Apple computer users.) But otherwise, at least one of these options should have you speeding through the Web faster.

Happy surfing! ■

Making the most of the Net

A Carnegie Mellon Institute study recently found that for 169 people in Pittsburgh, more hours spent on the Internet meant slightly more depression and loneliness. At about the same time, a study of 1,000 Michigan adults for the Michigan Information

Technology Commission found that people who use the Internet are more likely to be outgoing in the rest of their lives. They're the kinds of people who go to movies rather than rent videos, for example.

I'm not a social scientist. But it seems to me that these two studies may actually be in agreement. What if folks who are naturally outgoing are more likely to use the Internet?

If they spend a lot of time on-line, they might feel a little cut off from the folks with whom they usually hang out. Because they're outgoing people, that might make them a little depressed. But at the same time, they still might be more likely to go to movies, attend church or go out with friends than their less-social counterparts.

If both studies are right, they still don't answer the question of whether depression is a serious problem or just the to-be-expected result of changes in the way people spend their time.

If the studies do contradict each other, it might be that we're talking about two different groups of people. Many of the families in Pittsburgh took up the Net for the first time during the study; they were new users. Many of the folks in the Michigan study may have been using the Net

for a while, judging from their acceptance of things such as buying goods on-line.

In my experience, when people first use the Net, they are fascinated by the on-line social scene of chat groups and e-mail. After a while, the glamour wears off, and people steer away from chat that wastes their time and discard discussion groups that have become inane.

They start to use the Internet as a tool: Hop on-line for some Web information. Check the e-mail to see whether the kids wrote. Keep tabs on a discussion group or two devoted to something of interest.

It's possible that as people's needs for the Internet change, it starts to affect them in a more positive way.

Want to skip as quickly as possible to that stage? From years of experience visiting chat rooms, discussion groups and information sites on-line, I have a few tips on how to use the Internet most efficiently to enhance your daily life:

DON'T USE CHAT ROOMS TOO OFTEN. Some are a lot like some teenagers' phone calls: pointless and time-consuming. The same goes for some newsgroups, the virtual bulletin boards of the Internet, where folks pop in from around the world to post

messages on every topic imaginable.

DO USE E-MAIL DISCUSSION GROUPS. Because you have to subscribe (at no cost) to so-called "lists," they tend to be filled with people seriously interested in talking about the subject at hand.

DON'T HESITATE TO USE THE WEB AS A REFERENCE BOOK. Need a recipe for salsa? Want to find out the deadline for getting into that community education class? That's what the Internet does best, and research is often quick and easy.

DO USE THE NET TO COMMUNICATE WITH PEOPLE YOU KNOW AND LOVE IN REAL LIFE. It's amazing how easy it is to send a few lines of e-mail to someone you don't have time to call. And person-to-person instant messaging, or Internet phone software, can cut down on those long-distance bills.

DON'T SACRIFICE YOUR REAL LIFE FOR THE NET. The people you meet on-line are nice and rarely the raving maniacal pedophiles you read about in the news. But you're almost never going to form the strong bond of mutual experience with them that you can with friends and relatives. ■

INSIDE

E-mail

Being polite: Basic Netiquette

Judging from the response to a column on urban legends, stories that take on a life of their own on-line, it's time for a new Internet e-mail commandment.

What are the e-mail commandments? I'm glad you asked.

1. Thou shalt not spam. Sending a cute joke or sales pitch to 50 of your closest friends may seem like a good idea. It's not. They're already getting cute jokes and sales pitches from 50 other friends and will regard your mail as one more reason to stop writing to you.

2. Thou shalt not SHOUT IN ALL CAPITAL LETTERS. If hitting the shift key really slows you down, go for the e.e. cummings style and put everything in lower case.

3. Thou shalt not send large attachments. Even if the person on the other end really wants to see what you have to send, you may torpedo his e-mail account if you send files that are too large.

For pictures, reduce the resolution, size and color depth to make them very small. For programs, ask first; better yet, just send a link to the file's location on the Web.

4. Thou shalt avoid sarcasm and irony. Tone of voice is everything in subtle humor, and that's exactly what gets lost on the Internet. Even your closest friends may take that joking e-mail as a sign of your real feelings. It's better to avoid the confusion. (Adding extra smiley faces doesn't help.)

5. Thou shalt not flame. It's tempting, when people post something you strongly disagree with, to attack the intelligence (or lack thereof) that led them to spout such nonsense. It's even more tempting to slam people who do rude things — including breaking these commandments.

Don't.

Explain politely why you feel the person is in the wrong, if you must, but avoid any speculation as to his origin or character.

6. Thou shalt not bank on immediate responses. Don't e-mail people expecting that they'll read your note posthaste, even if they have done so in the past. Drawing their attention that way to something that's happening now may be an exercise in frustration for both of you if the message doesn't get delivered in time.

Call, visit or send an instant message with information that needs to be delivered right away.

7. Thou shalt not copy big quotes. Many e-mail and newsgroup packages default to quoting the entire message you're responding to in your reply.

Learn how to turn that feature off, and copy and paste just the part of the other message that you need to respond to. There's nothing more annoying for people in a list (e-mail) or newsgroup discussion than to see you post the entire text of a lengthy message, followed by two new words: "I agree."

8. Thou shalt not re-forward. If you've gotten a message that someone else has forwarded to you, and you decide to send it along to someone else, be kind. Open the original message and forward that — not the message that your friend sent you (which contains the message you actually want to forward).

This avoids the "Russian doll message" phenomenon, where you have to open the message inside the message inside the message to see what someone really wanted you to read.

AND OUR NEW COMMANDMENT:

9. Thou shalt not forward stories, virus warnings or calls to action without looking for them first in an urban legends archive such as **www .urbanlegends.com**.

(**NOTE:** I asked readers for their suggestions for commandment No. 10 and was swamped by responses. Here's the column that followed:)

If there were an e-mail purgatory, my readers would cheerfully fill it.

Responses poured in from all over to my column about the nine e-mail commandments. Here are some of your suggestions for commandment No. 10:

From Sue McGrath of Lake Orion, Mich., who says she loves e-mail: Thou shalt not besmirch, badger or otherwise abuse friends and relatives who do not have e-mail.

From Phyllis Snow of Grosse Pointe Farms, Mich.: Thou shalt keep it short.

From Diana Cheney of Farmington Hills, Mich.: Thou shalt use spell-check before sending.

"I am probably the only person that this bothers," she says, "but it is my No. 10 anyway." Take heart, Diana. You weren't the only person to send this in. Just ask Barb and Ed Taylor of Ann Arbor, Mich.

From Vincent Woods of Rochester, Mich.: Thou shalt always use an informative subject line.

From Randy (Josh) Emmett of Royal Oak, Mich.: Thou shalt not go on-line and make fun of people's names. ("How rude!")

From Jim Ponder of Warren, Mich.: Thou shalt not use fonts in very light colors, such as pink or yellow, especially when combined with a different-colored background.

From Paul Streby of Flint, Mich.: Thou shalt not send e-mail to an entire discussion group when thou needest only e-mail one person from the list.

From Jim Rudolph of Petoskey, Mich.: Thou shalt be sure of who thou art replying to.

From John Hebert of Chesterfield Township, Mich.: Thou shalt be extremely careful when sending the identical personal message to multiple addressees. (He goes on to describe painful office gossip that was mistakenly addressed to the subject.)

From Nancy Colina of Grosse Ile, Mich. (with a strong second by Joseph L. Fromm, former mayor and current resident of Grosse Pointe Farms): Thou shalt not forward chains. If it is encased in a very nice message that you wish to forward to friends, thou shalt cut and paste, thereby removing the veiled threat of good or bad luck.

From T.M. Reese of Brighton, Mich.: Thou shalt not Reply if that's not what you're doing. Instead, thou shalt hit Compose Message. Also, thou shalt delete the list of previous recipients that clutters up the tops of messages you forward.

From Barbara D. Malone of Oak Park, Mich., an assortment: Thou shalt not ...

... continue to send photos and attachments when the receiver has expressed no interest in receiving them.

... get angry when replies are not made promptly or at all.

... take every word so seriously.

From Paul Schmidt of Grosse Pointe Woods, Mich. (and others): Thou shalt not forward e-mail with addresses included.

From John Balough of State College, Pa.: Thou shalt not bear false witness against your fellow Netizen by falsifying your From: line or pretending to be someone else.

From Joseph McCluskey of Seattle, our runner-up for best new commandment: Thou shalt use the subject line wisely. ("Thou shalt not use large signature files is a stand-by for No. 10," he says.)

AND OUR WINNER,
a combination of Netiquette and common sense from Charles J. Stivale of Ferndale, Mich.: Thou shalt never e-mail anything thou wouldst not want thy mother to read. ∎

Urban legends

Are the offers piling up in your e-mail box almost too good to be true?

Recently, in messages sent along by readers who were genuinely trying to keep me informed, Microsoft offered me $5 for forwarding e-mail, Bill Gates and Walt Disney Jr.

offered me a free trip to Disney World as part of a joint promotion, the Gap offered me free clothes, and Gerber baby foods offered me money if I could produce a child born in the right year.

I would have been much more excited by it all if I hadn't been so concerned about the state of the world today — and the state of the Internet.

I read that CNN had reported that calls to Internet service providers were going to have surcharges. Or was it that every piece of e-mail was going to be taxed? I can't remember. To tell you the truth, I'm so worried about partying with people I don't know and waking up without a kidney or flashing my headlights at the wrong car and getting shot that I just can't remember much.

Because you all wouldn't have sent me those messages if they weren't true, right?

Welcome to the world of urban legends. I get a dozen new ones in my e-mail box every week.

It used to be that you could easily spot an urban legend, an outlandish story that gets told until it takes on a life of its own.

Would someone really have the forethought to bring along surgical tools on a date to harvest your kidney and then leave a note written in lip-stick telling you to call 911? I mean, get real.

But the folks who create these legends have been getting craftier. The stories are starting to take on an air of normalcy, even familiarity.

The people I've had to write to recently, gently letting them know that they have sent me a modern-day fairy tale, have been chagrined. Gee, they say, I wouldn't have sent it, but the note was from a trusted friend ... and it said that CNN or the New York Times or NBC or (fill in your trusted media outlet here) said that it was true.

So how do you tell whether you're reading the truth?

BEWARE OF ANY MESSAGE THAT INSTRUCTS YOU TO SEND COPIES TO ALL YOUR FRIENDS. Most legitimate organizations don't want their messages forwarded just anywhere. It will make the messages look like spam — or urban legends.

DON'T TRUST A MESSAGE THAT TELLS YOU TO TAKE ACTION. This is especially true if it cites a legislative bill number or a news agency, and you can't verify that bill or news report yourself.

Check media Web sites. Many papers post their stories. Going to lists of state and federal bills, you might find that the bill numbers cited in these messages don't exist.

IF YOU'RE STILL NOT SURE, START SEARCHING FOR THE STORY AT ARCHIVES OF URBAN LEGENDS. Try the easy-to-remember **www.urbanlegends.com** .

DO WHAT YOU WOULD DO IN REAL LIFE: PICK UP A PHONE AND CALL SOMEONE WHO WOULD KNOW. Urban legends about Internet fees have become so common that the Federal Communications Commission has taken to debunking them on its own Web site: **www.fcc.gov** . The agencies cited in the message will know whether the cause is for real.

FINALLY, IF IN DOUBT, DON'T. Don't answer the message. Don't send the money. And, for my sake, don't forward the e-mail to everyone you know.

I have yet to see a true e-mail asking for national support or action. Throw your resources behind causes you care about in real life; leave the legends to die a quick death on-line. ■

E-mail discussion groups

People on the Internet talk to one another about rock bands, English tea and dripping faucets. They hold lengthy discussions on Louis Tiffany glass, carburetors for '65 Mustangs and the newest episode of "South Park."

If you want to get off-the-cuff advice and companionship from folks interested in the same stuff you are, the Net is the place. And one of the best ways to find those kindred souls is to join a mailing list, sometimes called a Listserv after the trademarked software that runs some groups.

Unlike other types of discussion groups on-line, list messages arrive in your e-mail box each day. You subscribe to a group (free) by sending an e-mail, and you quit the same way.

Every list is run by a single computer attached to the Internet. That computer uses software to keep track of a roster of people who are interested in discussing a particular topic. That's why it's called a list; the computer is just keeping track of a list of names and e-mail addresses.

Because lists are a little harder to manage than things like chat rooms or newsgroup discussions, they're often more exclusive and of higher quality. It's harder for salespeople or someone feeling snotty to drop in on a list to post an offensive message and leave.

The level of maturity among the folks discussing your topic varies from list to list, however; you may want to try out a group or two before you decide which lists to stay on.

Here's how they work:

To add yourself to the list of people interested in a topic, you send an e-mail message to the computer running the group and ask to subscribe. You get a message back from the computer with some welcome information, including the e-mail address with which you can send messages to the group.

Every time someone sends a message to the list address, it's forwarded to everyone else in the group. If someone wants to reply, he sends that message back to the list address, and the reply is forwarded to everyone. The result is that throughout the day, messages will pile up in your e-mail box as people talk about the list topic.

How many messages you get a day depends on the list. Some lists have only a posting or two a month. Others have hundreds a day. You can always quit if it gets to be too much.

It's important to note that there are TWO e-mail addresses at work in a list: the administrative address of the computer (where you send messages asking to join or leave the group) and the list address (where every message is forwarded to the other members).

You have to be careful which address you send mail to. If you send a command (like subscribe or unsubscribe) to the list address, the computer won't read it, but will instead forward it to the group.

On the flip side, if you send a message intended for the group to the administrative address, you'll get an error because the computer will try to obey your command and get confused.

So how do you find the list for you? One of the best Web sites to search for lists is Liszt, at **www.liszt.com** . Type a key word or two and see whether it pulls up any groups that talk about what you're interested in. If it does, it will give you complete instructions on how to join.

Liszt is not a complete catalog of every mailing list on the Internet, so if you don't find exactly what you're looking for, you might try subscribing to something close.

That way, you can ask the participants in that list whether they've heard of any other groups discussing exactly what you want. (Can't find a group on tea roses, for example? Try subscribing to a general rose or gardening list and asking around.)

Once you decide to join a group, Liszt will give you instructions on where to send your subscribe message and what to say inside it. The computer that runs the group will send you a welcome message with the list address. It'll also have instructions on how to get off the list later, so SAVE THIS MESSAGE.

After that, it's a piece of cake.

The messages will come in like regular e-mail, and your replies will be forwarded to everyone else in the group. ■

Filing incoming e-mail

Computing is the only skill where the more experienced you are, the more likely you are to drown — in e-mail, that is.

In the last section, I recommended joining lists: discussion groups whose messages come to you via e-mail. Every other Web site you visit offers you the opportunity to get updates or product information or daily tidbits in your mailbox. And if you've been using the Internet for a while, you probably already have a healthy group of people to whom you talk.

So what do you do with all that mail?

There are two tricks that most e-mail programs will allow that may keep that steady flow of messages under control. The first is to create folders where you can file read and unread messages until you get to them. The second is to filter incoming mail directly into those folders, so you don't have to read messages right away to know what they're probably about.

Start by making folders to file your mail. Don't automatically divide them arbitrarily by subject or by who sends them. That's one way to divvy up your messages, but you might also want to divide messages by why you read them. For instance, you might put the mail from all your home improvement lists in one folder, even though one has people talking about plumbing and the other about the best time to trim your roses.

Once you've made a list of all the folders you might want, it's time to tell your e-mail program to make them. To make folders in Outlook, for example, you click once on your Inbox to select it, then click on File, then New, then Folder. To figure out how to make folders in your e-mail program, use the Help menu and search for the word "folder."

Once you've got the folders made, moving messages is often as easy as dragging them to the folder you want or clicking on a File in Folder button.

Now you're ready to tackle incoming mail. Eudora, Netscape, Outlook, Pegasus — virtually every e-mail program — includes a way to filter incoming mail. You're telling the program to look for a word or address in the header or body of the mail. If it finds that key word, it moves it to the folder you want.

In Netscape, you'll find this feature under the Mail Filters menu option. In Microsoft's Internet Mail, you'll look for Inbox Assistant. And in Outlook, you'll look for Rules Wizard. Search your mail program's Help menu for "filter" to get specific instructions.

(If you use Outlook 97, you'll need to upgrade free to Outlook 98 to use this feature. Check the Microsoft Web site, **www.microsoft.com/outlook** . Outlook Express users don't have this problem.)

Say you decide you want all the messages you get from Aunt Sylvia to go into the Family Mail folder you created. You'll make a new rule, telling your mail program to look in the "From:" line of incoming messages. If it finds Aunt Sylvia's e-mail address, the rule continues, the program should move the message to your Family Mail folder. You'll make a different rule for every type of mail you want to move.

Filters help most when you have lots of discussion lists coming into your mailbox.

Sometimes it's hard to see what's your personal mail and what's just part of the ongoing discussions. By filtering each discussion group or combination of groups into its own folder, you separate those messages out from the important personal items. You can read about stained glass or mountain biking or fat-free cooking when you have time and still see right away when an important message has come in.

Finally, a filter can help get rid of junk mail. You can tell it to look for the address of people who have sent you ads or questionable messages in the past. If it finds those addresses, it can filter those messages to a Questionable folder — or straight into your Deleted Items folder. ∎

Junk e-mail

There's a new bible for Internet users: "Stopping Spam" by Alan Schwartz and Simson Garfinkel.

You're going to love it.

If you've been on the Net for longer than a month or two, you know the heartache of spam. Useless, unsolicited messages promising everything from hot sex on-line to a million dollars in 10 days pile up in your mailbox. Responding to them just gets you more junk mail; the return addresses are often bogus.

After 20 minutes of reading "Stopping Spam," I had a dozen pages marked for later use. After two hours, I quit marking them; they're ALL that good. "Stopping Spam" (O'Reilly, $19.95, **www.ora.com /catalog/spam** or 1-800-998-9938, 9-8 weekdays) came out in 1998, but it's still a great overview of how bulk e-mail and newsgroup postings work, how this horrible trend got started and what you can do about it.

Schwartz and Garfinkel have a clear, entertaining writing style that all of us can read, regardless of our technical experience.

The advice runs from basic to highly esoteric, including a chapter for people who run e-mail systems. Still, you'll never have problems following along, thanks to careful explanations of terms and some great real-life analogies.

For instance, the authors compare the dialogue that two computers have passing along e-mail on the Net to the dialogue you have when you call up a restaurant to make a reservation.

The book begins by detailing why spam is such a huge problem. It's more than an annoyance; it's a threat to the usefulness of the Internet and a drain on the resources of every service provider.

Spam was first predicted by an Internet pioneer in 1975, long before most of us were aware the Net existed. His descriptions of how unwanted messages would annoy were grim but accurate.

The book details several high-profile early spams. (Remember the "I have a great collection of child pornography" messages? Or the lawyers who advertised their representation in the green card lottery on every newsgroup on the Net? Consider yourself lucky if you don't.)

In plain English, the book tells how to avoid and

eliminate e-mail and newsgroup spam.

The suggestions include how to protect your e-mail address from getting out in the first place, how to tweak your e-mail filters to intercept incoming spam and how to use spam bait pages to add to spammers' burdens.

The authors talk about how to find out where the message really came from and how to complain effectively to the companies that give the spammer Internet access. (Spamming violates most Internet providers' contracts with their customers, so complaining can make the bulk mail stop coming.)

Finally, they go over software that may help you de-spam, most of which is cheap or free.

Schwartz and Garfinkel wrap up by considering long-term solutions to spam, from Net community action to legislation.

The bad news is that getting rid of spam isn't easy, and this book doesn't gloss over the difficulty. The good news is that it contains the tools to drastically cut down on the unwanted mail or postings you have to read. ∎

Confessions of a spammer

I have a confession to make. After years of crusading against junk e-mail, I have apparently become my own worst enemy. I'm a "spammer" — a sender of junk mail — at least in the eyes of America Online.

It all started when I decided I was tired of having a bunch of work-related mail on my home PC. I didn't want to kill the mail and didn't feel like making the effort to save it to disk, but still wanted to be able to get it from the office.

So I forwarded the messages, about 150 in all, to my AOL account. I reasoned I could pick them up when I got back in the office.

It wasn't long before the nasty messages started arriving. AOL's automatic e-mail monitor had discovered my nefarious actions and had blocked all those messages. I was banned from sending e-mail to any AOL user. In short, I had spammed myself.

Oh, the shame.

My first response would have been to laugh, except that this is the on-line service famous for its junk messages from outside mailers and AOL itself.

Two of my friends have used AOL's preferences to cut off all mail from outside addresses in an attempt to cut down on the junk. I actually gave up and abandoned one screen name and created another in an attempt to flee the garbage.

So AOL, despite everything from lawsuits against spammers to these automated messages, can't seem to cut down on the hundreds of e-mail ads I get. But it certainly can intercept legitimate messages, each different, from a single e-mail address to my single e-mail address. How maddening.

Fortunately, my time in purgatory was short. It was less than 24 hours before I was again able to send mail to myself and (gasp!) other AOL users. Repeat spammers, according to AOL spokesman Rich D'Amato, are banned forever. But to give more specifics on how AOL controls incoming mail would just invite true spammers to circumvent the system, he said.

"AOL is using all technological means at our disposal to protect our members from spam," he said.

Regardless of whether you use AOL, you can try some strategies to cut down on junk mail.

First, my friends don't have a bad idea. If you have an AOL account, going to your Mail Controls and turning off mail from outside sources may send those businesses enough bounced e-mail notices that they'll quit sending junk.

Be sure to set it up so that mail you do want will still get through. You'll have to type in each address you still want to hear from.

If you don't have an AOL account, follow this simple rule for cutting down on the junk: Keep a low profile. If you post a message in an Internet newsgroup or Web-based discussion group, you WILL get junk mail.

If you're visiting a Web site (or are an AOL member) and are asked to put together a member profile that other people can look at, you're asking for those direct mail marketers to read and make note of your address.

If your e-mail address is included in a directory, you're a target for junk.

When you join an e-mail discussion group, be sure you read the introductory message to see whether your name and address are in a public directory somewhere. Follow directions to erase yourself from that roster.

FINALLY, DON'T REPLY

to those offers to remove you from the junk mail distribution. Many unscrupulous companies just take that as proof that your address is good. ∎

How to send attachments

The yen to send something snazzier than letters and numbers strikes quickly after you start using e-mail. Most e-mail programs let you send and receive almost any kind of file with your mail, so you can enhance your words with pictures, music or movies.

Files sent with e-mail are called attachments. Many e-mail programs use a paper clip icon for the buttons to attach a file or for incoming mail with an attachment.

Sending an attachment requires just two simple steps: telling the program that you want to attach a file to your outgoing e-mail and showing the program where the file is. You'll take those two steps while your new e-mail is open on the screen, just after you've finished writing the message.

In Microsoft Outlook, just hit Insert, then File in the menus. A dialogue box will pop up and ask you to identify the file you want to send. Use the drop-down menu at the top of the box to choose the drive where the file is, then double-click on the folder on the drive where the file is stored. Once you see the file, double-click on it and you're done. Send the mail.

In Netscape, click on the icon of the paper clip in the tool bar of the message you're writing. Choose File from the menu that pops out and pick what you want to send.

When you send files, remember that not all people can read files from all types of programs. If you've just finished laying out your newsletter in PageMaker, for example, you may not be able to send that file to someone else to look at unless the other person also has PageMaker.

You may be able to get around that by using the File, Save As function to save a copy of your document in a format your friend can read.

Warning: If you get your mail from a free Web service or from Juno, you may not be able to handle attachments. (Juno requires a Juno Gold account, which costs $2.95 a month.)

Here's an example of sending an attachment, in this case photos:

If you've scanned in a picture or drawn something in a graphics program, the first thing to think about is what file format you should use.

The same picture can be stored by your computer in a bunch of different ways, and how you save it can make it easy or difficult for the person on the other end to get it open.

Because you're sending your picture over the Internet, you'll probably want to save it as a JPEG (JPG for non-Apple computers) or GIF file. These are acronyms for two common types of graphics files that are used extensively on the World Wide Web. Nearly all Web browsers (like Netscape or Explorer) and many e-mail programs can open these files.

Saving your artwork in one of these formats is easy. When you're done scanning or drawing, click on File, then Save, as usual. When the dialogue box pops up and asks where you want to save the file, pick a folder where you'll be able to find it later.

Usually, there will be a line in the dialog box that says something like "Save File As Type" with a drop-down box. Click on the down arrow or triangle and you'll see a list of every format in which your program can save files.

If you can't find JPEG or GIF, the next-most-common file type is a Windows Bitmap file, or BMP. (If you're a PC person sending a picture to a Mac person, or vice versa, try a Tagged Image File format, or TIFF.)

Pick your preferred format out of the list by clicking on it. Your program may add the file extension automatically — that is, it may add a .JPG or .GIF to the end of the file name. If it doesn't, type it in yourself. It helps Windows PCs figure out what kind of file it is dealing with.

Another bit of good advice comes from readers and advisory board member Marcie V. Smith. She and others noted that if you want to make your scanned photo easy to send and receive, be sure to set your scanner to read the photo in low resolution (say 72 dots per inch, the standard resolution on the World Wide Web).

You can also reduce the size of the photo file by cutting the number of colors it has. Many scanners default to 16 million colors. If you reduce that to 256, you won't see much difference in quality on the screen, but you will see a big difference in file size.

All right, now you've saved the file in a format that people can read. Fire up your e-mail program and compose a message to the person to whom you want to send the picture. Then follow the directions at the beginning of this section to attach the file. ∎

Attachments you receive

So you've sent a piece of e-mail with the photo or artwork as an attachment. Now it's time to handle an attachment that someone else has sent to you.

In many e-mail programs, you can tell when there's an attachment to a note that's waiting for you because there will be a picture of a paper clip next to the message in your list of mail or inside the e-mail itself.

To get at that artwork someone sent you, you're going to have to download the attachment, that is, store it on your machine where other programs can get at it to read it. Typically, you'll just click on the paper clip or Attachments button while you're reading the message.

A note for America Online users: Opening attachments is one area where AOL really shines. If someone has sent you a picture in the .JPG or .GIF formats, AOL will open them for you automatically when you read your mail. If you want to save it for later, you can choose to download the attachment. The dialogue box will look a lot like the ones other folks get when clicking on the paper clip.

The dialogue box that pops up on your screen if you click on the paper clip or Attachments button (at least for Windows 95/98 and MacOS) should look familiar. It's the same kind of display you get whenever you go to save a file in any program. At the top of the box, you'll see a drop-down box with a downward pointing arrow or triangle that lets you pick the drive or directory where you want to save the file.

Be sure to pick somewhere you'll remember later! If you don't want to save the file permanently, you can always stick it on your desktop, so you can find it easily and drag it to the Trash or Recycle Bin.

Toward the bottom of the dialogue window will be a line asking you to name the file. Sometimes file names get garbled when people attach things to their e-mail messages, so you may need to rename it something understandable. If you're working on a PC, be sure to keep the three-character file name extension — the letters that come after the period — the same. That helps Windows figure out what kind of graphic or document it is.

Once you've saved the file, you need to open it, sometimes using a different program. If the people who sent the picture used .JPG or .GIF formats, you can open it using Netscape or Internet Explorer. If you've saved the graphic to your desktop, that's easy: Just click on the graphic and hold down the left mouse button. Now, still holding down the button, drag the file over on top of the Netscape or Explorer icon and let go. The program will open and will show you the graphic automatically. (You can print from there, too.)

If you saved the picture somewhere else, open the program you'll use to look at it. Then click on File, then Open (or Open Page) and tell the program where to find the graphic you saved.

If the person sending you the pic-ture did not use one of these two common formats to save their file, you may have trouble opening it. Try opening the file using a graphics program, a layout program or a good word processor, if you have one. (Read the directions in these programs for how to place or open graphics.) These programs can often open some pictures.

If that doesn't work and you're unsure what type of program was used to create the graphic, take a look at the file name. If it ends in a period and a few characters, you may have a clue. For instance, .ai files are pictures drawn using the Adobe Illustrator program. Files ending in .doc were probably created using the word processor Microsoft Word.

If you're trying to open the file by double-clicking on it in Windows, be sure to take the check OUT of the box that says "Always use this program to open this type of file." If you guess wrong, you don't want your computer to try that program with this type of file again.

For a complete list of all common file extensions — those characters after the period at the end of the file name — and which programs typically make those files, check out **www.whatis.com** on the Web and click on "Every file format in the world." If you have the program that was used to make the picture, you'll be able to open it.

As a last resort, you may have to ask your friend to save the photo or drawing in a different format and send it again. ■

INSIDE

The Web

Guessing addresses

Sometimes you don't want much out of the Internet.

A fact, a phone number, a single picture. You may want to hop on, pick up a tiny bit of information and quickly hop off. You can do that, of course, unless you don't know the address of the site that has what you need.

How do you get that address? Try these steps:

GUESS. It helps to know how Web addresses work. Commercial sites tend to end in ".com," federal government sites in ".gov," Internet provider sites in ".net" and nonprofit sites in ".org." Add a "www." and the name or an abbreviation of what you're looking for, and you may get there: **www.ibm.com**, for example, or **www.census.gov** or **www.unitedway.org** .

State of Michigan departments tend to start with "www." and end in "state.mi.us." So the Michigan Department of Education is **www.mde.state.mi.us**, for example,

while the secretary of state is **www.sos.state.mi.us** .

But what happens if you type in **www.aaa.org** and instead of getting the American Automobile Association, you get the Amateur Astronomers Association of New York? Time to start using more sophisticated tools.

WHOIS. Network Solutions, the company that registers private Web addresses for the United States, will allow you to check its records to see what domains — basic Net addresses like freep.com — are registered to a company or person. The search is crude, but often effective.

Visit **www.networksolutions .com/cgi-bin/whois/whois** and type in American Automobile Association. You'll get a list of 10 sites registered to companies like that one, including the one you're looking for: **www.aaa.com** .

Click on the name of the site to get the address, phone number and, often, the e-mail address of the person who registered the site.

YAHOO. Still no luck? Your next best bet is a search engine compiled by people in which Web sites are listed according to categories. Yahoo, **www.yahoo.com**, is the most popular. Type Detroit Free Press into the search box on that page and you'll get a list of matches, including our main page at **www.freep.com** .

For southeast Michigan sites, check out **www.alldetroit.com** .

ALTAVISTA. But what if you're looking for a single person's page, not some big business? Visit a powerhouse computer-compiled search engine like AltaVista: **www.altavista .com** . Because AltaVista's main catalog is put together by machines instead of people, there aren't nice category listings for every site. But there are many pages to search through.

If typing in the name of the person or company gets you too many matches, click on the link that says "Advanced" and type your new search into the larger box that appears on the page.

Most main pages for people and companies are going to include their names right up in the title. So you can type "title:" and the name to narrow your search to just pages that list the name that way. For instance, searching for `title:"traffic jam & snug"` (the quotes tell Altavista this is a phrase you want to keep together) will bring up a list including **www.traffic-jam.com**, the Web site of the Detroit restaurant.

If you know you're looking for a government or nonprofit site, you can tell Altavista you want only addresses ending in, say, ".org." To do that, include `url:.org` as one of your search terms. (URL, for Uniform Resource Locator, is just a fancy term for a Web address.)

METASEARCH. No luck? Try a search engine that compiles the results from a bunch of search sites together. You won't have as much control over the search, but you will get a lot of results. One favorite is DogPile at **www.dogpile.com** .

NEWSGROUPS. Finally, you might stumble across a site if someone else is talking about it in a discussion group. DejaNews archives many newsgroups, or discussion group, messages. Try searching for your person or organization at **www.deja.com** .

If you get what looks like one of the individual pages posted by that person or company, look for a link to the home page, and if you don't find one, check out the address: Chances are, you can remove everything after the first slash and get back to the main page. ▪

Using search engines

You've wandered into the world's largest library, and it looks like the aftermath of a tornado. Books are strewn everywhere, articles are piled in random heaps, and the card catalog is a hopeless mess.

Welcome to the Internet. This global computer network has officially become the fastest-growing repository of information the world has ever seen. Unfortunately, the custodial staff appears to be on vacation, and the reference librarians are having a hard time keeping up.

So how do you find anything in this mess? Search engines.

Search engines are necessary because virtually everyone who has an Internet account has some small bit of space to store World Wide Web pages or other information. That's what makes the Net such an incredible library: People around the globe can post tidbits about what interests them without needing the kind of cash that paper publishing requires.

But this very flow of information is what makes it so frustrating to try to find something in particular on the Net.

Those people don't have to tell anyone what they're doing or submit a summary of postings for some master catalog. And with thousands of new items on the Net every day, it gets complicated to keep track of new postings.

That's where search engines come in.

In a nutshell, a search engine is a Web page that allows you to look for other Web pages. Each search engine assembles its own, continuously updated catalog of Web pages from around the Net and attempts to help you find the ones that cover the topic you want.

To use a search engine, you visit that engine's Web site, then either click on subject headings until you find the pages you need or type in a few key words to do a direct search of the engine's catalog.

Without search engines, the only way you'd find anything on the Web is through recommendations from other people or dumb luck.

There are two main flavors of search engines: those built by people and those built by computers. People-compiled engines have human beings reviewing every page before it goes in the catalog.

"Oh," the reviewer might say. "Here's a page on interest rates. I'll put it in the finance section, under the banking heading, in the interest rates category."

Those humans find pages through a bunch of fairly technical ways, most of which involve scanning known Web master sites for new entries.

When you visit a search engine compiled by people, you're likely to see a list of subject headings on the Web page. If you clicked on Finance, then on Banking and finally on Interest Rates, you'd see a short summary of the page the reviewer found and the Web address where you can find the page.

This is the advantage of using people-built search engines. Every page has been looked over by human eyes, and finding something that you're interested in by category is a lot easier than thinking of the right key words for a search.

The drawback is that because people have to look over every page, people-built catalogs tend to be a lot smaller. No one search engine of any type includes every World Wide Web

page, but people-built catalogs tend to be much smaller than their computer-built counterparts.

The most popular people-built search engine in the world is Yahoo, at **www.yahoo.com**. If you visit, you'll see a friendly list of subject headings. Click on a broad subject, such as Business, and you'll be taken to a list of smaller topics under that heading. Keep drilling your way through menu after menu and eventually you'll (you hope) find exactly the page you're looking for.

Computer-built search engines have tiny pieces of software whose job it is to search the Internet day after day for new pages. When a search engine finds a new page, it saves a text copy of it in its catalog. It doesn't read it or attempt to figure out its subject category.

When you visit a computer-built engine, you type in a key word or two, and ask the site to search its catalog looking for those words. If the software finds your key words in a Web page, it will show you the title, the first 30 words or so on that page and the address where that page can be found.

The disadvantage is that searching like this is much more difficult than using headings, and you may get more hits than you bargained for. The advantage is that because the catalogs for these search engines are much larger, you have a much better chance of finding lots of pages that match your interests or of finding that one page you're looking for.

Some of the most popular search engines on the Web are compiled by computers. Northern Light, at **www.northernlight.com**, and AltaVista, at **www.altavista.com**, are two of the largest.

Though these virtual reference librarians will never finish stacking all those heaps of documents in neat piles, they can at least point you to the few they've found that you might be of interest to you.

You can aid your search at computer-compiled search engines by using their advanced search pages and some common search terms.

Anyone who has gone to a computer-compiled search engine has had the same bad experience: You type in your key search words and are told they match 400,000 documents.

Getting the four documents you really need takes a little extra thought. Let's take the example of AltaVista.

If you decide to use AltaVista to research your upcoming vacation to Colorado Springs, you might be tempted to type the key words `colorado springs hotels` into the first search box. Your results: 504,000 matches. Ouch!

AltaVista, like most major search engines, uses a very quick search for people who visit its main page. It looks for any one (not all!) of your key words in a Web page, and if it finds any matches, it shows them. It tries to put the best matches on top.

Here's hint No. 1: Always look for a link — one of those underlined blue words or graphics that you can click on — that lets you do an advanced search. Many search engines have them. Usually, advanced searches let you tell the computer at the other end EXACTLY what you want.

Hint No. 2: If you use a search engine a lot, READ THE DIRECTIONS. There will always be a link from the search page that lets you click for instructions. On AltaVista's Advanced Search page, it's the link marked Help.

On AltaVista's Advanced Search page, you learn, you can use the word "and" to tell the computer that your matches must contain ALL of your search words instead of just any one. So without reading the rest of the help pages, you rush off and try: `colorado AND springs AND hotels`. The results: 1,566 matches.

This is better, but still too many to handle. Returning to the help pages, you see that you can use quotes to force AltaVista to show you pages where only some of your words appear as a phrase. So now you try: `"colorado springs" AND hotels`.

Better still. Now you're down to 673 matches. Now what if you had a way to force AltaVista to put the city and hotels near each other? Upon visiting the help pages for the last time, you see that you can, in fact, use the word NEAR to put your keywords within about a sentence of each other.

Now you're ready. You type: `"colorado springs" NEAR hotels`. Bingo! You get just 40 hits, and right in the Top 10 are the Colorado Hotel Directory and the Bed and Breakfast Country Inn Directory.

And instead of sifting through thousands of Web pages, you spend your next five minutes reading about snow-capped mountains.

AN UPDATE: AltaVista has begun to incorporate more intelligent search technology into its quick-search page, so you'll get fewer results from that page now than you used to.

Still, using advanced terms like these will get you directly to what you want, with fewer hits, at AltaVista and other search engines. ∎

Find your way back to favorite sites

Cruise the Internet for long and you start to bury your desk in scraps of paper.

You cover envelopes, sticky notes and torn corners of whatever is handy with the Web addresses you've found and want to visit again. Fortunately, there is an easier way.

Bookmarks allow you to save the address of a page you'd like to visit again so that you never have to remember it or type it in. Get good at organizing your bookmarks, and you'll have handy lists of sites on all the topics you want to read about.

The directions here are for Netscape users, but Microsoft Explorer and other Web browsers do the same thing. Consult the Help menu in your program.

When you visit a page that you'd like to get back to later, bookmark it. Make sure the page you want is up on the screen. Then click on Bookmarks, Add Bookmark. The next time you click on Bookmarks, you'll see the title of this page at the bottom of the list. No matter where you are on the Web, you can click on that item in the list to take you right back to this site.

Bookmark enough pages and you'll have a list that stretches down past the bottom of the screen. Even worse, your bookmarks about stained glass will be mixed up with the ones for football scores, making it hard to find the one you want.

Don't despair! You can change the order of your bookmarks and group them into folders. Here's how:

Click on Bookmarks, then Edit Bookmarks. A new little window will pop up with your bookmarks inside, but now you can edit what's in the list. To delete anything you don't want, click on it ONCE to select it, then tap the Delete key.

(Double-clicking on the bookmark will take you directly to the site rather than just selecting it.)

To change where the bookmark falls in your list, click on it and hold down the left mouse button. Now drag it to wherever you want it to go. When you get it where you want it, take your finger off the mouse button to drop your bookmark there.

You can organize your bookmarks into folders to keep similar pages together. To create a folder (still in the Edit Bookmarks window), click once on the line at the top of your bookmark list. It will say something like "Heather Newman's bookmarks."

This tells Netscape that you want to put your folder in the main list. (You can also put folders inside other folders. That's why it's always good to create a folder at the top of your bookmark list, so you don't create folders in odd places.)

Now click on File, then New Folder. The new folder will appear. Type in its name, and hit the Enter key. Your folder is now ready to hold bookmarks. To move bookmarks into the folder, use the same technique you used to move them around: Click once on the bookmark, hold down the left mouse button and drag the bookmark up until the folder is highlighted. Then drop it.

You can tell what bookmarks are in a specific folder because they'll be connected directly to the folder with tiny dotted lines.

You can make as many folders as you like. To delete a folder you don't want, just click on it once to select it, then hit the Delete key. (Warning! All the bookmarks inside that folder will also be deleted. If you don't want that, drag them somewhere else first and make sure the folder is empty.)

When you're done editing your bookmarks, click on File, then Close. This little window will disappear. Now when you click on Bookmarks, you'll see your new folders with all your favorite Web sites inside. ∎

How to download files

Saving information from the Internet's World Wide Web can be a trick. Now you see it, now you don't.

Maybe you clicked through all the correct steps to save a file, but can't find it on your hard drive. Maybe you're not sure how to get it from your screen to your machine. We'll talk about both steps here.

Saving files from the Internet (also called downloading) is a useful thing to learn. It also lets you tap into the Net's endless supply of information and free and almost-free files — software, clip art, screen savers, you name it — and save it for future use.

There are a couple of ways to preserve items from the Internet on your hard drive.

The first works when you see something on your screen that you'll need later but don't want to print out.

To get your Web program to save the page, check under the File menu. In Netscape, the command you want is under File, Save As.. . Other browsers have similar commands. When you click on Save As.., Netscape is going to ask you where and how you want to save this page.

At the top of the Save As.. box, you'll see the folder where Netscape will save the page next to a little label that says Save In:. To change the folder, click on the down arrow button next to it.

You'll see a list of all the drives on your machine (the floppy, your CD-ROM, the hard drive). Click on the one where you want this Web page to

be stored, then double-click on the folder in which you want it.

Now the folder is displayed next to the Save In: label. Your second choice is how you want to save the file.

At the bottom of the box, you'll see a label that says Save File as Type: next to a white box. Click the down arrow button attached to this box and you'll usually get two choices: HTML (*.htm) or plain text (*.txt).

If you want to look at this page again later using Netscape, choose HTML by clicking on it. If you want to open it later with a word processor, pick plain text.

Finally, name the file using the File Name: space in the middle. If you picked HTML format, make sure the file name ends in .htm; if you picked text, make sure it ends in .txt. This will help Windows figure out what

kind of file this is later when you open it.

Click on the Save button in this box and you're done. A copy of this Web page is now in the directory where you told it to go.

The other way to download information can be used when you can't see the file you want on the screen because it's not a Web page. This is true of every program you might find on the Web.

When you click on the file name, the Save box comes up instead of a new Web page.

The Save box looks just like the Save As.. box from the first method. Change where you want the file to go, but DON'T change what type of file it is or the name. Programs often won't run if you don't download them as-is. When you click on the Save button in the box, you'll see a progress bar — a little window that tells you how the saving process is going. When it disappears, the file is downloaded. ■

Using downloaded programs

OK, so you've found that perfect computer program on the Internet and downloaded it to your PC.

Now what?

Using My Computer or Microsoft Explorer in Windows or Finder on a Mac, find the directory where you put the file. Its name should end in a period and two or three letters.

If you don't see ANY file names with a period and these letters on a PC, Windows is hiding them from you. Go to My Computer and open the directory you want to see. Click on the View menu item in that window, then on Options. In the new window that pops up, click on the View tab. You'll see an item that says Hide MS-DOS file extensions. Click in the box to get rid of the check mark. Then click OK.

Now you should see all the file extensions, the characters that computers use to help themselves figure out what kind of files they're dealing with. Seeing the extensions helps you, too, because if you know what kind of file you've got, you'll know how to handle it.

Follow these steps:

1. Copy the file to its own directory.

Programs and zipped files can be made up of more than one smaller file, and when you inflate everything, you don't want to lose those files among the ones that are already stored in an existing directory.

2. Inflate it if it's a zipped file.

Large files, such as pictures or programs, can take a long time to download from the Internet to your computer. So people who post those items sometimes try to make it easier for you by compressing the size of the file. The most common PC-style compression results in file names that end in .zip, hence zipped or ZIP files.

To inflate those files back to normal size after you've downloaded them, you'll need an unzipping program. One good option is WinZip, which you can download and try out free. (Find it by searching for WinZip at **www.download.com**). It's shareware, so if you like it, do the computer world a favor and send the programmers their small fee.

Put WinZip into its own folder on your hard drive. (To do that, open My Computer, double-click on the picture of your hard drive and click on File, New, Folder.) Drag the WinZip installation file into that folder and double-click on it. After it installs, it will automatically link itself to files that end in .zip. So the next time you download a zipped file and double-click on it, WinZip will run automatically.

(StuffIt is one of the more popular compression programs for Apple computers. Files created with it end in .sit. You can find StuffIt

Expander at the same Web site, and it runs in much the same way.)

2A. Look at the files you get after your downloaded file been inflated for something like setup.exe or install.exe. Double-click on that file.

If you don't see a file named setup.exe or install.exe, look for a readme.txt file and double-click on it to open it; it usually has instructions.

3. If the file name ends in .exe, double-click on it. The program will either start to run, or you'll see Windows inflating compressed files. If you see Windows inflating files, go to step 2a.

4. If what you downloaded wasn't a program after all — you've inflated it, but there are NO files ending in .exe — check the Web site to see whether there's a better description of what the file contained and how to use it.

That's it! You've successfully downloaded a piece of software and run it on your computer. ■

Cookies

Cookies on your computer are just like cookies in real life: A few are great. More than a few can be a problem.

Computer cookies are tiny bits of text that remember things you did or information you entered while visiting a Web site.

There are two kinds: temporary (or session) cookies and permanent cookies. Session cookies are almost always harmless. They live only during the time you're on-line on a particular day and disappear afterward.

Permanent cookies are recorded in a file or folder on your hard drive (cookies.txt for Netscape users in Windows, the Cookies folder under the Windows directory for Explorer users). If you have trouble finding the files, search for cookie* under Start, Find, Files or Folders.

What you'll see is mostly garbage: the address of the site that set the cookie, followed by a string of text characters. These are codes that the site uses to remember things about you.

The good news is that cookies can generally only be read by the site that set them. That means that one Web site can't see what you've been doing or buying on another. The exception to this rule is banner advertising.

Because one company (DoubleClick, for example) often places banner ads on a number of sites and because those ads are also capable of setting cookies, ads are theoretically capable of tracking your movements between sites.

Fortunately, you can control how your Web browser uses cookies. In Netscape, hit Edit, then Preferences. On the left side of the screen, click on the setting Advanced.

You'll see several choices: accept all cookies, accept only cookies that get sent back to the originating server, disable cookies and warn me before accepting a cookie.

In Explorer, you can choose to allow, disallow or be prompted to accept both permanent and temporary cookies. See Tools, Internet Options and Security; then click on Custom security settings.

In either program, accepting all cookies means that any time you visit a site, it has the capability of storing information about you in that file or folder on your hard drive. It can't read anything else stored on your computer.

If you choose to be notified every time a site wants a cookie, be prepared to be annoyed. Many popular sites use them, and some use more than one.

The third option in Netscape is more flexible: It limits cookies to just the site that originally sent them. This helps foil the banner ads from following you from one site to the next and allows you to enjoy cus-

tomized pages without security worries.

There are legitimate uses for cookies. If you customize a site, setting a weather page to display your area or a movie times page to display the theater near you, your preferences are often recorded in a cookie.

That way, the next time you visit the site, you see the information you asked for.

One thing you can do periodically is sift through your cookies and throw out the ones you don't need. Despite what the heading says at the top of the Netscape cookies.txt file, it's just a plain text file and won't be hurt if you edit it. Just make sure that you remove whole lines at a time.

You can delete individual cookies from the Cookies directory for Explorer with no ill effects. In either case, you can see what address the cookie hails from and whether it's one you want to keep or jettison. ■

Sites to visit

The Top 10

To get you started, here are my top 10 Web sites to visit:

1. Northern Light Search: **www.northernlight.com**
My favorite Web search engine, because of its well-organized results pages and folders and because of the incredible size of its catalog.

2. BigBook: **www.bigbook.com**
I use this collection of Yellow Pages to search for businesses within a few miles of my home. It's much quicker than checking multiple print phone directories.

3. Learn2: **www.learn2.com**
This site gives quick summaries of new skills, from darning a sock to making flavored vinegar. It tends to be earthy, easy and fun to read.

4. The Dollar Stretcher: **www.stretcher.com**
Tips and hints on how to live better for less — definitely my mantra. There's a great e-mail newsletter to sign up for here.

5. MapQuest: **www.mapquest.com**
This is the site I turn to when I need to give someone directions.

6. Inns and Outs: **www.innsandouts.com**
A terrific directory of bed and breakfasts everywhere in the country.

7. TechWeb's Encyclopedia: **www.techweb.com/encyclopedia**
Think computer writers always know what those acronyms stand for or how ISDN lines work? No way. We visit TechWeb and look up the terms we need to know about in the encyclopedia search box. A terrific tool.

8. Ziff-Davis: **www.zdnet.com** (also CNet news, **www.news.com**)
This collection of magazines has searchable archives on-line that make it easy to learn about anything related to computers. And CNet offers great computer news on-line that is updated constantly.

9. Edmunds: **www.edmunds.com**
Absolutely everything related to cars: new car prices, used car prices, specs, dealer's invoice costs, you name it. Visit here before you go buy.

10. Detroit Free Press: **www.freep.com**
OK, so it's a blatant plug. But I firmly believe we're the best Michigan news on the Web.

TWO BONUS SITES:
MerriamWebster has put its dictionary online at **www.m-w.com** . And at **www.voycabulary.com** , you can even type in a Web address and get every word on that page hyperlinked to its definition. The Web page looks just as it did before, but every word is clickable. ∎

Finding old friends on-line

You've read the Freep, slapped the Spice Girls and shopped for CDs on-line. You're bored with the Internet and looking for something new. How about tracking down some long-lost buddies?

The Internet is a storehouse of national and international phone directories, e-mail listings and other nooks and crannies where you can attempt to track down long-lost friends from high school, college or kindergarten. Here's where to start:

If you were to pick up the phone and ask directory assistance for a national or even state-wide search on your friend's name, you'd be laughed off the line. But dozens of Web sites will let you try just that. Two of the best are InfoSpace (**www.infospace.com**) and Switchboard (**www.switchboard.com**). Plug in your friend's name, and you'll get phone numbers, addresses and even opportunities to send a card or flowers.

A caveat: InfoSpace and Switchboard are based on white pages from around the country that have been retyped by hand. Switchboard is updated quarterly, spokeswoman Elaine Haney says. InfoSpace's director of business development, Chris Matty, says his directory is updated monthly.

They get their information after another company has had the time to type it in. (In a spot check of some Free Press names, we found some recent changes that were already in the directories, but others had been out of date for two or three years.) Of course, unlisted numbers will not appear.

What if your friend lives abroad? Try two international directory collections, at **www.teldir.com** and **www.springboard.telstra.com.au /directories/global.htm** .

You also can learn whether the Web page for your college or high school offers a directory of alumni. (An off-line tip: Many college alumni offices will forward a letter to the student's last known address if you send a request, a blank envelope and postage.) Look for your school on-line at Yahoo's education directory: **www.yahoo.com/Education** .

If you were in a fraternity or sorority together, try to track your friend through the national organization. Find a directory at **www.greekpages.com** .

Another way to find old school pals who are on-line: Search a site such as Classmates, **www .classmates.com**, that helps reunite alumni. Registration is free and allows you to search a database of students from more than 30,000 schools in North America.

No luck there, but still convinced your friend may be on-line? Check a great e-mail directory like Internet Address Finder at **www.iaf.net** . This directory is compiled mostly from Web postings, discussion group messages and other databases. On America Online, search the Member Directory (key word: Directory). Or try InfoSpace's e-mail directory, at the address above.

Your friend may have posted something in a newsgroup, one of the discussion groups on-line. Search for mention of your buddy in a newsgroup message at **www.deja.com** . Also don't forget to use traditional search engines such as Northern Light, **www.northernlight.com**, to learn whether your friend's name pops up in a Web page. Heck, he may even have posted a page looking for you!

If the person you're looking for

was really, really, really into the Grateful Dead or tea roses or backgammon, you might find him lurking in the newsgroups or e-mail discussion groups devoted to that topic. Find out how to visit those groups at **www.tile.net** .

Think your friend may be a lawyer? Check Martindale-Hubbell's Lawyer Locator at **www .martindale.com/locator** or West Legal Directory's search at **www.lawoffice.com** . A doctor? The American Medical Association may have her in its directory, at **www.ama-assn.org/aps /amahg.htm** . (Careful, that hyphen is important.)

One great resource to find retired members of the military is Military City, at **www.militarycity.com /newsroom/registry.htm** . ■

Customize your Internet

The World Wide Web is getting smaller — in one way, at least.

Numerous sites have taken steps to let you customize what you see on-screen when you visit. That makes the amount of unwanted material you have to slog through on a page shrink dramatically.

If you aren't using these custom tools, you should be. Here's how:

First, pick an entry point onto the Web. Your browser's home page — the Internet site you see when you start up — can be changed to whatever address you'd like, say **www.freep .com** to make the Free Press home page your starting point.

But don't stop there. You can customize your view of individual information pages.

For instance, do you want REALLY detailed local weather? Visit the Weather Channel at **www.weather .com** and click on Customize My Weather. You can set what cities you'll see, what maps you'll get — you name it.

Or if you're an eBay addict, you can see all the items you've bid on (or are selling), your feedback and even links to your favorite categories of items up for auction. Head to **www.ebay.com** and click on My eBay.

You may have noticed that visits to technical support pages at sophisticated sites like Microsoft's result in automatically customized pages. The site uses cookies (remember them?) to remember what you searched for the last time you came by and stands prepared to show you that kind of information on that topic or program again.

There's even a tool to assist you if you don't want to customize what pages show you, but rather what pages you see. QuickBrowse at **www.quickbrowse.com** will save lists of Web addresses and send you the actual pages, collected together into a single e-mail, as often as you like.

The links will work, you'll see the pictures, and you won't have to hop from page to page because they all will be in a single piece of mail. If you'd rather see them put together on the Web than in your e-mail box, you can do that at the site.

Many banks and brokerages now offer custom pages for their customers that show real-time account information (protected by a secure server and a password).

Ask your credit card company, broker and banker what they can offer.

Web portals such as My Yahoo! at **http://my.yahoo.com** also gather information and let you customize how it appears on your screen; check your favorite home page for details. ■

Recipe & cooking sites

In the fall, a young woman's fancy lightly turns to thoughts of food — especially when the aroma of someone else's Sunday dinner invades a three-mile run on a brisk autumn afternoon.

So when I get home, I head straight for the kitchen — and walk through it to the office, to fire up my computer.

When I think of food, I think of the Internet.

This isn't just because I'm a hopeless computer geek. I've simply learned from experience that if I want a recipe for something, the Internet is the best place to go.

Even if you never visit your kitchen except to microwave life back into a cup of cold coffee, you can find directions to the food of your dreams on the Net.

The best place to find a recipe is arguably the Searchable Online Archive of Recipes, which is run out of the University of California-Berkeley Web site. You can find it at **http://soar.berkeley.edu /recipes** .

It has more than 37,000 recipes for everything from Tibetan steamed dumplings to Southern fried turnips. You can choose from general categories or type in a few key words to search for a dish. I typed "honey mustard dressing" and came up with three recipes; a search for "apple pie" yielded more than 30 versions.

Another great site is Flora's Recipe Hideout: **www .floras-hideout.com** . This recipe catalog isn't as big, but its contents are yummy. This is where I found my own special recipe for low-fat brownies. (Shhhh, don't tell anybody.)

The main page usually has tidbits on fixing a particular dish, and at the bottom, you'll see headings for various types of food

There's also some general kitchen help that could come in handy.

Flora's site is part of a so-called recipe ring, which is a group of Web sites that have chosen to link to one another. You can go from one site to another in the group by clicking on

the icons at the bottom of each page.

If you're more the outdoors-with-fire type, you need to check out "BBQ in Cyberspace," an amateur but excellent rating of barbecue sites, at **www.iPass.Net/-lineback/bbq /links.htm** .

You'll find links to the thousands of recipes at the Hot and Spicy Cooking Page, the On-Line Recipe Archive of the BBQ Internet Mailing List and the Internet Barbeque Review of BBQ restaurants.

For those who prefer to sit back and let someone else do the cooking, there are a few good Detroit and Michigan dining guides on-line.

Check out **www.justgo.com /detroit** and click on Dining to get to starred reviews of Michigan restaurants, complete with hours, location, a description of the cuisine. The list is searchable by area, meal and type of food.

Last but not least, don't forget to check out the Detroit Free Press Web site: **www.freep.com** .

You can search for recipes you saw in the newspaper or restaurant reviews by clicking on "Search," then typing in the name of the recipe or eatery. Or visit the food section at **www.freep.com /index/food.htm** . ∎

Fitness & sports sites

Lose weight. Get fit. Learn a sport.

If you're like me, resolutions like these usually last as long as leftover Christmas cookies. Lucky for us, there are sites on the World Wide Web designed to encourage folks long on ambition and short on willpower.

First up, two sites that focus on my sport of choice: running. The premier listing of everything having to do with running in Michigan is RunMichigan!, at **www .runmichigan.com** .

It has race results, often posted the day of the event. You'll also find a calendar of things to come and club information that is guaranteed to get you out on the street.

For a national perspective on running and cycling, check out Do It Sports at **www.doitsports.com** .

You'll find advice columns, profiles on national events and results for everything from track and field to downhill mountain biking.

Walkers can get their fill at Ruth's Power Walking Page, at **http://members.aol.com /PowerWalkr**, which includes race pictures, cross-training advice, tips and travelogues.

If you're trying to get into those snowy seasonal activities, check out the mecca of skiing info at **http:// skicentral.com** . It has a daily ski guide, links and resort information on about 600 centers, including two dozen in Michigan.

Skaters can hit the ice at **www.icesk8.com** , which includes

everything from skating art to links to a competition guide.

If you'd rather stay indoors, there are excellent sites on bodybuilding and fitness put together by exceedingly enthusiastic trainers and experts: **www.atozfitness.com** has links and articles on bodybuilding, exercise and nutrition.

Fitness Online has a pile of links to better exercise and eating habits at **www .fitnessonline.com** .

Some sites include information about supplements, so don't forget to check with your physician before radically altering your diet or your exercise program.

Yahoo offers links to the stuff that's good for you — such as exercise and diet tips — at **http://dir.yahoo.com/Health /Fitness** . For every sport under

the sun (and some that aren't), check the list of sports links at **http://dir .yahoo.com/Recreation/Sports** .

On the eating end of things, a nice collection of low-fat food tips, recipes and links can be found at **www.kitchenlink.com/health** .

You'll find links to fitness and food calculators, health organization sites and virtually every other type of fitness or healthy-eating Web site you can think of. ■

144

Tax & finance sites

Let's explore a few Web sites that offer to guide you as painlessly as possible through the annual task of figuring out what you owe your Uncle Sam.

First on the list is an excellent tax planning guide put together by accounting firm

Deloitte & Touche, at **www .dtonline.com/taxguide98 /cover.htm** . The company also has a useful site for general financial planning, but the tax site is especially helpful.

A host of pages detail the 1998 changes in the federal tax law, at least one of which will probably affect you. There are tips for planning during 1999, and the company includes links to updated tax information as it comes out each year. The tax info for the 2000 filing season will probably appear close to the end of 1999. Topics are explained in understandable language.

The Deloitte & Touche site includes advice on planning to minimize future taxes, fill-in interactive tax worksheets (how much will you owe?), a tax calendar, tax rates table, retirement plan limits, the tax effects of gifts and a mileage deduction table.

If you want a computer to prepare your return and don't have a lot of specialized forms to file, you might want to consider TurboTax Online at **www .webturbotax.com** . The same easy question-and-answer format included in the TurboTax software is available to anyone who can use a Web browser.

You won't find the sophisticated planning tools or exhaustive library of forms that you do in the TurboTax program and you won't find its excellent library of books included in the program.

But you will be able to prepare your basic return, with the most common supplemental forms, for $9.95, including electronic filing (which speeds your refund, if you're getting one).

Hugh's Calculator site includes a pile of calculators that can help you spare a bit of your income from Uncle Sam. Find it at **www.interest.com /hugh/calc** .

Ernst & Young puts tax tips, tables and forms on-line at

www.ey.com/tax . It's not as detailed as the D&T site, but does offer some different information and a nice collection of tax cartoons.

Both Ernst & Young and mutual fund company T. Rowe Price, at **www.troweprice.com/iranew**, offer interactive worksheets that help you figure out whether it's better to invest in the traditional, tax-deductible IRA or in the Roth IRA, which doesn't give you a tax deduction up-front but does give you tax-free money after retirement.

The worksheets also help you figure whether it's worth it to roll over existing tax-sheltered IRAs into a

Roth (since you have to pay taxes on the money to transfer it).

T. Rowe Price's site includes a retirement planning worksheet, which helps you figure out how much money you need to save for your golden years. See **www.troweprice.com /tools** .

At **www.taxnews.com** , Price-WaterhouseCoopers offers the Tax News Network for professionals — for a $450 annual fee — but gives lists of tax-related Web sites free if you click on the Tax Sites link.

The IRS offers answers to the most frequently asked questions at **www.irs.ustreas.gov/prod /tax_edu/faq** . An even better feature is its Tax Trails, a series of interac-tive pages that asks you questions and uses your answers to tell you whether certain things are deductible or whether you need to pay certain kinds of taxes. Find it at **www.irs .ustreas.gov/prod/ind_info /tax_trails** .

The IRS also is the authoritative source for original tax forms on-line. Check out the IRS's helpful main page at **www.irs.ustreas.gov** . In addition to lots of advice and links, the page also has a link to all the tax forms you'd ever need, which you can print and use.

Be warned, though: To see the chapters of IRS documents, you need to have the ability to read Portable Document Format files, which usually requires the Adobe Acrobat plug-in for Explorer or Netscape. The Web site has links to more information about Acrobat, which is free.

(IRS forms are also generally PDF files, so you're going to have to deal with Acrobat sooner or later.)

Schmidt Enterprises has links to all things tax, including a series of tax tips sites from around the country, at **www.taxsites.com/help.html** . Even better is TaxWeb at **www.taxweb.com**, which has links and original information relating to everything from forms to discussion groups to tax calendars, enforcement, news, filing locations, refunds, state taxes and organizations. ■

Free stuff

One of the best things about the Internet is the amazing variety of software, clip art and screen savers available free (or next to it).

Shareware, or software that you use BEFORE you decide to pay for it, is available in amazing quantities on the Net.

One of the best shareware archives for all kinds of software is CNet's shareware.com, found on the Web at **www.shareware.com** . You can search for programs by type and many come with instructions. Or try ZDNet's **www.hotfiles.com**, where you can find picks from some of the country's hottest computer magazines.

If you like a program, don't forget to send in your check! Otherwise, the programmers may stop distributing their work free. Most programs include information on how to pay under the Help menu.

Check out **www.screensavers .com** for a collection of (you guessed it) screen savers, and **www.clipart .com** for a collection of free icons and graphics. ■

Can you trust the web?

What should you believe?

People who think the Internet is dangerous for unsupervised children picture their tots wandering among predators and pornography.

But there's a danger that's much more common, one that every youngster on the Net sees every time he or she logs on.

It's context — or, more accurately, the lack of it. I know that sounds terminally dull, but stick with me for a paragraph or two.

The Net is the world's largest library. But unlike most physical libraries, it doesn't limit itself to works prepared by knowledgeable adults.

Instead, the Net is more like a vast crowd of people from around the world, each shouting that he is telling the truth, the whole truth and nothing but the truth. That's terrific when it gives you and your kids a chance to hear different points of view, especially from folks you wouldn't usually read or see in the news.

But it also means that you have to greet every piece of information on the Net with skepticism. After all, it's difficult to be sure who posted the facts that litter millions of Web sites and thousands of discussion groups. Did the military really shoot down TWA Flight 800? Are two virgins really going to consummate their relationship in cyberspace?

Experienced journalists for bigcity newspapers — a Parisian journalist in the first example, me in the second — swallowed those two bits of Net nonsense hook, line and sinker. And we're supposed to be trained to winnow out the fake stuff.

You may be better at figuring out what's a hoax than we were. But what about your children? The Net bombards them with information that may not be true.

Do they have the skills to puzzle out what's real, what's biased and what's fake? Or will they believe that women steal men's kidneys in hotel bathrooms, that Neiman Marcus charges $250 for a cookie recipe and that the Holocaust never happened?

Even if they're reading nothing but the truth from carefully selected Internet sites, are they equipped to cope with those facts that fly at them with no context and no explanation?

At best, their experience is like coming in at the middle of a movie and trying to figure out what has already happened. At worst, it's like hearing different groups' propaganda delivered in the soothing voice of Walter Cronkite. On the Internet, every Web site can be an authority.

So what can you do?

At home, follow the same steps you take to protect your children from other dangers on-line. Put the computer in a public place where you can keep an eye on what they're reading. Talk to them about what they've seen and help them ask questions about who's presenting the material. Is this somebody they've heard of outside the Net?

Let them know that just as in the real world, people lie on the Net and that they shouldn't believe everything they hear. If they have questions, encourage them to come to you to check things out. Suggest alternate sites where they can look up information on the same topics, sites that you have checked out.

Finally, consider talking to your school principal about the idea of including some of this instruction in your child's social studies or English classes. Critical thinking has been an educational buzzword for decades. As more and more schools give their students access to the Internet, it's going to become essential that children learn to question and judge what they find there. ∎

Shopping on-line

You're missing out on some great deals if you're on-line and not shopping.

But in survey after survey, some folks say they use the Internet to window-shop, then head to their local stores to buy. They're worried about giving their credit card number to companies they don't know and can't see when it comes time to dispute a charge or make a return.

The Net is a fabulous place to window-shop. Most manufacturers have Web sites where you can get product information. Plug the manufacturer's name into a search engine such as **www.google.com** . Automotive sites, such as Edmunds (**www.edmunds .com**), can provide useful background, such as how much the dealer paid for your car.

Merchants who use the Internet to sell their wares enjoy the same advantages as mail-order companies: no showroom to lease and stock, fewer salespeople to pay and lower overhead as a result. It can pay to buy stuff on-line.

So how do you get comfortable with shopping on the Internet?

Start by learning about security. Encrypted sites scramble information that is passed over the Net so that your credit card number isn't traveling unprotected. You can tell when you're visiting a secure, or encrypted, site by looking at the bottom left corner of your Web browsing software.

Netscape and Explorer both have a symbol to show you whether a site is secure. It may be a key or a padlock. When it's connected and shining, you can be sure that the site is using encryption. In both programs, you can also click on that icon for more information about the site's security.

If you want an extra measure of protection, download and use the 128-bit encryption version of your software from the Netscape (**www .netscape.com**) or Microsoft (**www.microsoft.com**) Web sites. Both Netscape and Explorer offer this version, which is legal to use only in the United States. (The encryption is so difficult to break, compared to the regular 40-bit version used in standard releases of the programs, that it's considered cryptography and therefore a potential war-time tool. So it's illegal to export the software.)

NEVER give your credit card number to a site that is not secure. The chance of your number getting hacked on its way to the company is slim. But if a company won't pay for the technology to encrypt its servers, it's not serious about doing business on-line.

Once you've found some good secure sites, start by buying items that are identical regardless of where they're purchased. This is why pages like **www.amazon.com** and **www.cdnow.com** are so popular: They sell books and CDs, two items that are mass-produced. Other examples might be printer cartridges, computer components, software or airline tickets.

Because these items are all alike, you know exactly what you're getting.

Once you're comfortable with a site and its quality, you can start to get more adventurous.

Start small with a new site. You'll pay a little more to ship just one item, but you'll find out just how fast the company is with delivery and how good its customer service really is. If the first order goes well, you can buy with more confidence.

Always use a credit card rather than sending in checks or money orders. If you're actually ordering on-line, a credit card is often your only option. But some companies will let you send in money the old-fashioned way. Avoid it. Using a credit card gives you protection if the company doesn't ship what it promised. You can dispute the charges, and if your card number is stolen, you're liable for only $50.

Check the company out. Most firms will tell you where they're based, and you can call that area's Better Business Bureau. Search for the company name in the archives of computer news reports and computer magazines at **www.zdnet.com** and **www.news.com** to see whether it has made a splash in the on-line community.

Don't be afraid to use that ability to challenge. Regardless of warranty, companies on the Net, like firms everywhere, should deliver what they promise when you pay for the merchandise. If you don't think you got what you paid for, use the card company as your ally. Call your credit company for instructions.

Print out the order screen before

you send it in. It may be the only record you have of your purchase. If you see a confirmation screen, print that out, too, and file it until you receive both the merchandise and your credit card bill. Finally, copy any information the company lists for its address and phone number right on the printed bill. That way, you'll have them if you need them, even if the Web site comes down.

For any major purchase, ask the company for referrals to people who have bought from the firm before. If you're buying something specialized, you might consider checking an on-line "list" e-mail discussion group for people who would be potential customers of that company to see whether they've ever heard of it. For instance, if you're interested in buying stained glass materials, you might check with members of one of the Net's many stained glass lists.

If there's anything that doesn't seem right to you about the company or its Web site, don't buy. The old adage applies: If it seems too good to be true, it probably is.

Finally, take a deep breath and do it. The risk that someone will steal your card number and charge items is one you take every time you give your card to a waiter or shop clerk. You'll love the convenience of ordering simple items on-line. ■

Using on-line auctions

My name is Heather, and I am an Internet auction addict.

(Hello, Heather.)

It's been 10 minutes since I've been on-line.

It all started so innocently. I'd been on the hunt for a particular type of '50s glassware and I thought: "Hey, what about that great eBay on-line auction site (**www.ebay.com**)? Maybe it'll have a piece or two."

It did have a piece or two. Plus a thousand pieces or two to go with it. Sellers from Sarasota to Saskatchewan were touting their wares, and all I had to do to find the exact thing I was looking for was to search for a couple of key words or to browse the right categories.

I knew on-line auctions were a hip place to hang out. EBay alone has more than 2 million items up for bid at any given moment in auctions that usually last about a week.

But I thought I could handle it. I didn't think it would be this much fun.

I was wrong.

I was searching for Fire-King, a kind of post-World War II Pyrex. I was rewarded with the descriptions of thousands of objects, platters and pitchers and Primrose plates.

That was the beginning of the end.

To see an item up for bid, all I had to do was click on the description.

There, in loving color, was a photo of the piece and a detailed listing of its qualities and condition.

By clicking on the seller's name, I could e-mail a question about the object. By clicking on a number after the seller's name, I could see hundreds of feedback notes from previous clients.

Does the seller pack glass well? Ship promptly? Stand behind the merchandise? I could see it all at a glance. The site even summarized the comments (positive, neutral, negative) and assigned a ranking to the person based on those reviews. If a seller is going to cheat someone, he or she is going to get to do it only once.

On the flip side, there are reviews of buyers, too. Do I send my checks on time? Do I respond promptly to sellers' questions? It's all there.

(As if that isn't good enough, eBay offers $200 of free insurance, with a $25 deductible, for any buyer or seller who doesn't get his or her goods or money. If your item is more than $200, eBay offers information about escrow services that guarantee you won't pay without getting the merchandise. And it offers a way for buyers and sellers to verify their information through eBay, so others know who they're dealing with.)

If I decided I wanted the item, the Web site made it so easy . . . too easy. All I had to do was enter the maximum amount I would be willing to pay. That number was kept secret, and eBay would record my visible bid: 50 cents or a dollar more than the highest offer so far, depending on the price of the item.

The site would automatically bid against anyone else who wanted the piece until it hit my maximum. If no one else joined the fray, I paid only the amount of the initial bid. If someone else wanted the thing badly enough to really bid up the price, I would pay no more than my limit.

If someone outbid me on an item, eBay would tell me by e-mail so I could decide whether to raise my limit. If I won, it would tell me how to contact the seller and claim my prize.

Before I knew it, I had bid on dozens of items. I was distraught when I was outbid, elated when I won. It took days for me to reel myself in.

Now I watch patiently for the few pieces I really don't want to live without. Consider my tale a warning, my Visa bill a reminder of how you, too, can be sucked in.

You might think this is just the foible of a glassware collector, a hobbyist dabbling in areas you don't care about.

But what if I told you that on-line auctions feature everything from diamonds to Dodges to digital cameras? Books, movies, music, Beanies and baseball cards?

Master your maximum bids and watch your wallets, my friends. There's something in on-line auctions for everyone. If eBay doesn't float your boat, you might just find that perfect item at Auction Universe (**www.auctionuniverse.com**) or Yahoo (**http://auctions.yahoo.com**) or Amazon (**http://auctions.amazon.com**).

Then it might be you in front of your friends, with a living room full of merchandise and a guilty smile on your face.

Go ahead, repeat after me: I am an Internet auction addict ... ■

Children & predators

Sonia Hernandez picked up the phone, noting the number on her caller ID box. It was one she had seen displayed before, a friend of her daughter's. What surprised her was the deep adult voice she heard on the line.

"I asked him who he was," remembers Hernandez, who thought that he was a friend from school. She also questioned him about how he knew her daughter, who was just 13. This guy sounded much older. I'm not printing her daughter's name, at her request.

"When he told me he was 22, I said, 'Do you know how old my daughter is?' He said yes, that they had met on-line."

The dark side of the Internet had come calling, even though Hernandez, a Dearborn Heights, Mich., dental assistant, had done everything right. The family computer was in the kitchen, not in one of the kids' rooms. She was deliberately nosy.

"I walk by periodically and watch what they're doing," she said. "I keep track and I peek. I walk by and my daughter says, 'Do you mind, Mother?' I say, 'No, I don't mind at all.' "

The Hernandezes saved money all last year to buy their daughter and 15-year-old son a computer for Christmas. The day the kids opened the box, their parents set the rules: No porn. No giving the family address or phone number to anyone. The computer stays out in the open.

Hernandez said that she warned her daughter "about perverts and weirdos and how they try to lure you in. She's not ignorant."

So when Hernandez heard the man's voice on the line, it floored her.

"I figured he either had a screw loose or was up to no good."

She told him in no uncertain terms that he was not welcome. He was not to call her daughter, or write to her, or chat with her, or talk to her through her friends — ever.

"He apologized and said he wouldn't call again," she said. And he didn't. But after Hernandez found out the man had called her daughter's friends, she talked to their parents, and they laid down the same rules.

Her daughter was upset, Hernandez said.

"She said: 'Mom, he's a nice guy. He's my friend.' I said, 'You don't know anything but what he wants you to know.' "

The more they talked about the man, the more disturbing details she heard. When Hernandez's daughter and a friend had asked why the man was still living at home in New Baltimore, he said he was building his own house. He said he would build rooms for each of them, and they could come and live with him.

He asked the girls to meet him in person, again and again, alone or together. Thanks to all their mother-daughter talks, Hernandez said, her daughter resisted. It was the friend who gave the man the Hernandez phone number.

"Maybe it was harmless," Hernandez said. "It just didn't set right with me."

Her daughter was grounded as a result of the incident, and she has stopped talking to the man on-line. Hernandez even called the sheriff's office, but was told that unless the man had made sexual advances, he had not committed a crime. Hernandez will not forbid her children to use the Internet, even now.

"Computers are great. They serve a purpose. But they can be dangerous," she said.

Erin Diamond, a member of the Wayne County (Mich.) Sheriff's Department Internet Crimes Task Force, said that parents should learn about the Net, as Hernandez did.

"Have the child teach you how to use the computer system," he said. Parents should understand e-mail, chat rooms, the Web and how to use parental filtering programs. "As good a kid as you have, you don't know what people are sending you." ■

Filtering software

Parents worried about whether their children might see inappropriate information or pictures on the Internet have a powerful ally: their computers.

Filter programs work to block out potentially objectionable content, and depending on the package you install, they can also control access to anything from particular programs to the hardware settings of the machine.

We took a look at a dozen commercial filters that you can use at home; reviews of each are included here. You can also choose an Internet service provider that includes filtering capability within your accounts — with no need for your intervention.

To understand filter programs' strengths and limitations, you need a basic appreciation of how this software works.

Most filter programs intercept words on Web pages or other Internet content as it's on its way to your screen. They then compare that text to a stored list of naughty Web addresses, questionable newsgroups and chat rooms, and iffy key words.

If the text contains any of the objectionable information, the site is blocked before it appears on the screen. Typically, programs will block the entire page, displaying a warning that the site is inappropriate. Some filters attempt to filter out the individual offending words without affecting the rest of the content. Others prevent users from typing in forbidden words or phrases.

The best filters allow you to add or remove words and sites from the list of objectionable material so you can customize the filtering to your personal taste.

No matter how good the filter programs have become, most still rely on basic lists of key words or Internet addresses to do their job. That means that newer sites, which haven't yet been added to so-called bad lists, might slip through or that pages that contain innocent information might be filtered because they contain a so-called bad key word.

In virtually every case, the filter programs we examined fell down on the job of filtering some site they should or shouldn't have cut off. Installing a filter isn't a complete solution to all your concerns about Internet content.

"You can block all the sites you don't know about, but that's a lot," said Paul Resnick, a University of Michigan professor who helped develop the Platform for Internet Content Solution ratings used by many software packages and Internet Explorer. "You can let all the sites through you don't know about, but you'll let sites through you wish you hadn't."

In addition, there has yet to be a program made that couldn't be subverted by a determined teenager. Some teens have hacked into Department of Defense computers; a filter program may not represent much of a challenge.

Nearly all the programs we evaluated were password-protected once they were installed. To make sure that your children can't change your settings at will, be sure to pick a long password — containing both letters and numbers — that's difficult to guess and isn't made up solely of standard words.

Then be sure to remember it! Most of the programs required passwords to un-install, meaning that if you forget the administrator password, you might be in trouble if you ever decided you no longer want the filter to operate.

Small boys and girls are probably best off with a so-called positive filter, like Edmark's KidDesk Internet Safe. In those programs, you choose which Web sites or newsgroups or chat rooms are allowed.

For intermediate-aged children, who have more curiosity, need more freedom and are more likely to stumble across questionable content by accident, a full-featured filter program like Cyber Patrol might be the answer.

They're protected from most sites that would raise a red flag, you've got a lot of control over what's censored, and they're unlikely to dig too deeply to remove or reset the program.

For teens, you might be better off abandoning the policing aspect altogether and just spy instead. Cyber Snoop is one program that does an excellent job of running so transparently that your teen never needs to know it exists.

For additional information on Internet providers that offer filtered accounts and Web filter programs, see the Safe Kids site, at **www.safekids.com** .

WORLD WIDE WEB. The majority of what children look at on the Internet is this collection of text and photos posted on computers around the world.

NEWSGROUPS: These on-line discussion groups work like virtual bulletin boards, each on a different topic. Users can read what's been posted and make their own postings on discussions under way or new topics of their own.

INTERNET RELAY CHAT: These are channels of people discussing different topics 24 hours a day. Each line is displayed as soon as the person finishes typing it. IRC channels can be public discussions or private conversations between people.

FILE TRANSFER PROTOCOL: FTP sites exist solely to hold files that other users might want to download. Frequently, the programs or pictures that children might want to download exist on FTP servers.

INSTANT MESSAGING: This one-on-one paging service allows two people to chat directly or send messages to each other that pop up nearly instantly when both parties are on-line. Made famous by America Online, IM has been made even more popular by ICQ (I-Seek-You), a free program allowing IM over most Internet connections.

E-MAIL: These are text messages sent directly from one Internet user to another. They can also have attached files, which can be anything from another message to a picture to a program. Only a few filter programs track e-mail.

One option: If you're interested in filtering your children's Internet experience but you don't want to install software or put up with the potential inconvenience for your own surfing, you can buy them an account on a child-friendly Internet service provider.

Here's a look at a dozen popular filtering programs:

BAIR (BASIC ARTIFICIAL INTELLIGENCE ROUTINE) FILTERING SYSTEM: BAIR promises to do something that no other filtering system does: filter pictures. Most programs can examine only the text in Web sites, so if the site name is clean, the narrative is clean and the names of the image files are clean, the images are still displayed — regardless of what they depict.

BAIR did a reasonably good job at catching pornographic images. It filtered nearly every picture containing people, including many that were completely innocent. It let a few naughty ads and a couple of naughty pictures slip through.

BAIR also includes a key word filter that takes into account the context of the words in the Web page. It did a competent job of blocking most pornographic text, allowing just a few pages to slip through. It also blocked out some sites that have no sexual content, but had pictures of people or key words used in more innocent ways.

Filtering is controlled user by user and can be set to none, standard or ultra. The program filters only sexual content. Parents can purchase a separate ChildSafeMail account if they want key word and image filtering for their children's e-mail.

BAIR is packaged with access to Exotrope's excellent EdNet, a search engine of sites appropriate for children. Parents choose their child's grade level and search for topics.

The software works only with Internet Explorer (a version is included on the CD), and it filters only the Web. Operation was occasionally buggy, especially on pages that had lots of Javascript programming. The customized IE looks a bit primitive. It lacks time limits for young users or logging of visited sites.

BAIR (Basic Artificial Intelligence Routine) Filtering System; Exotrope Inc., **www.thebair.com** , 1-877-411-2247 (24 hours, seven days); $4.50 upfront, $6.95/month. Requires Pentium 90, Win 95/98, 16 MB RAM, 50 MB hard disk, Internet Explorer 4.0.

CYBER PATROL V.4: Cyber Patrol had the most flexible Internet content controls of any program we tested. It watches for violence, nudity, sex acts, gross depictions and text, intolerance, satanism, cults, drugs, militancy/extremism, sexual education, illegal acts, gambling, alcohol and tobacco.

A simple panel of radio buttons allows parents to choose whether children have full, filtered or no access to Internet Relay Chat, the Web, File Transfer Protocol, newsgroups, games or particular programs.

Cyber Patrol can keep track of up to 16 programs and limit the number of hours they are used each day. It logs when they are open. The time limits can be adjusted day by day, and the program includes a quick search for new programs that have been installed on the computer by adults or children.

Cyber Patrol uses Cyber NOT lists of sites, newsgroup names and IRC channels. In addition, key word filters can be used to block channels, newsgroups or Web sites by name. It tells you when its lists have been updated and allows you to punch a button to go on-line and get a new copy.

Chat Guard performs well at limiting what was typed from the keyboard or pasted from the clipboard; it's intended to restrict children from posting personal information.

The software uses encryption to protect files from hacking by children, and it allows you to set which user's preferences to default to.

Its major weakness is blocking sites, groups or channels based on their names, not on their content. It can allow some questionable sites with innocent names and addresses to slip through.

Cyber Patrol v.4; The Learning Company, **www.cyberpatrol.com** , 1-800-828-2608 (8 a.m.-6 p.m. Monday-Friday); $29.95 including three-month subscription to site lists ($5 more if you order by phone). Requires Windows 3.1/95, 486DX66, 8 MB RAM, 5 MB hard disk; or Apple 68040/33, System 7.1, 8 MB RAM, 5 MB hard disk.

CYBER SENTINEL 1.6: Cyber Sentinel did the best job of checking for naughty key words in a variety of programs beyond just the Internet. It caught bad words we typed into Microsoft Word, for example, and those displayed in newsgroup listings.

Parents can set what happens after a violation: any combination of a warning, the closure of the program or the capture of a picture of the offending information for the parent to view later.

The program uses a simple restrictive choice to pick how tightly you want content to be filtered. The program uses its own lists and yours. You can edit your own lists, but not the ones that come with the software.

Some filter companies consider the lists of blocked sites or words to be part of what sets their product apart, and refuse to display the lists for fear that competitors might copy their material.

Cyber Sentinel does not allow multiple settings for multiple users. It blocked sex sites, newsgroups and mail we tried to view. It did not block the innocent pages with questionable words we ran past it (the Traverse City Cherry Festival, a jar with a screw-type lid being sold on eBay).

It worked quickly and without major bugs.

Cyber Sentinel 1.6; Security Software Systems, **www .securitysoft.com/cybersentinel .html** , 1-888-835-7278 (9 a.m.-7 p.m. Monday-Friday); $29.95. Requires Windows 95/98/NT, 486 DX processor, 8 MB RAM, 20 MB hard disk.

CYBERSITTER99: A simple one-floppy-disk program, CyberSitter does a good job with the basics of filtering sites. It doesn't filter newsgroups, chat or FTP, but does allow parents to block those features altogether. It can be used to check e-mail, but is not recommended for any account where the user typically gets legitimate messages with attached files.

CyberSitter forces you to register the program to receive the lists of filtered sites and phrases, which may be a concern for families who normally would not fill out warranty cards as a violation of privacy.

You have the option of blocking access to selected Internet material, recording all violations and recording all sites visited. CyberSitter's lists help filter for sex, violence, gay and lesbian content, illegal sites, radical sites, hate, intolerance, cults, the occult, Web chat rooms, sports, leisure and Web advertising. It can automatically update its lists weekly.

You can add good sites, bad sites, words or phrases. It was effective at blocking the sex sites we tested and did not block innocent sites with questionable words. It does not support multiple users.

CyberSitter99; Solid Oak Software, **www.cybersitter.com** , 1-800-388-2761 (11 a.m.-7 p.m. Monday-Friday); $39.95. Requires Windows 95/98/NT, any computer.

CYBER SNOOP 3.0: Cyber Snoop was the best in our tests at running absolutely behind the scenes. If you're interested in quietly tracking what your teens are doing on-line without intervening in their choices, this is the program for you. The program tracks sites based on a list of allowed choices or a list of blocked addresses or key words that you compose.

It keeps a log of all sites, newsgroups, e-mail addresses, FTP sites and chat channels visited during a session by user, flagging those that violated the restrictions. Cyber Snoop can create a quick-link page of sites that were visited, so that you can click on each to see where your child has been. It can be set to block specific outgoing text to prevent the release of private information.

By default, Cyber Snoop displays no messages to your child, although it can be set to intervene or warn. It comes with instructions on how to disguise the name of the directory it's in on your computer, displays convincing system error messages when

actively blocking sites, and quietly turns e-mail into alphabetical garbage after it's sent if it finds restricted information inside. The program displays no icon, task bar block or easily decipherable file name while running.

Cyber Snoop 3.0; Pearl Software, **www.pearlsw.com** , 1-877-732-7579 (24 hours, seven days); $49.95. Requires Windows 95/98/NT, 486, 4 MB RAM, 10 MB hard disk.

DISK TRACY98: Disk Tracy includes both a Web filter and a utility to search the hard drive for stored material. It really shines during a hard disk search. During a search, depending on the options you choose, the program looks for pictures, compressed files or suspicious items. It scans text for sex, drugs, physically harmful or illegal activities and hacking. You can add a custom list of words to search for. It displays thumbnail-sized copies of all the pictures your children have been looking at and logs the sites they've seen on the Internet.

You pick the search depth you're interested in, or ask to have files that are less than a particular number of days old checked. In a search of our hard drive, it found text cached by our Web browser during previous testing sessions — not all of it, but enough to give Mom and Dad an idea of what the kids have been up to.

You can save search results and compare them with previous searches to see what has changed.

On the filtering end, Disk Tracy includes a fairly standard system based on site lists and key words to scan Web sites. Parents can also block FTP, newsgroups, chat or Web sites altogether, but can't filter anything but the Web. Users can customize site lists by adding or specifically deleting addresses, but can't

actually edit the lists.

The program can help generate an acceptable-use contract between you and your children.

Disk Tracy98; WatchSoft, **www.disktracy.com** , 1-888-709-2824 (9:30 a.m.-6:30 p.m. Monday-Friday); $34.95 (plus $3 shipping). Requires Windows 95/98, 486/25, 16 MB RAM, 18 MB hard disk.

KIDDESK INTERNET SAFE 1.0: Our pick for younger users, KidDesk creates a cute desktop for the child in your house, complete with the ability to send and receive text and voice messages to and from you and other users. It includes eight desk styles.

You customize the desktop by adding icons for programs and Internet sites you want the child to have access to. KidDesk comes with a link to specialized lists of kid-approved Web sites that you can easily add with a click. Your child must use KidDesk's own Web browser, which has limited commands, friendly buttons and is basically a modified version of Internet Explorer.

Each child in KidDesk gets his own desktop, settings, icons and password. You can prevent children from typing personal information into Web pages by blocking specific words.

The program comes with a helpful utility to list all the programs in your Windows 95/98 Start Menu to decide which to add to the desktop.

KidDesk is moderately secure, allowing you to specify that it be run on the computer's startup and that the computer shut down when KidDesk is shut down. Common keyboard shortcuts out of programs (Ctrl-Alt-Del, Ctrl-Esc) won't work when KidDesk is running. KidDesk is even friendly when you're getting rid of it; it offers to put all those icons you so painstakingly selected in a special group in your Start Menu.

KidDesk Internet Safe 1.0; IBM Edmark Software, **www.edmark .com/prod/kdis**, 1-800-320-8379 (9:30 a.m.-8 p.m. Monday-Friday); $29.95. Requires Windows 95, 486/66, 8 MB RAM, 8 MB hard disk, Internet Explorer.

NET NANNY 3.1: Net Nanny is easy to set up and understand and allows users to edit lists or import lists from other places. It gives parents the option of masking words, logging the hit, displaying a message or shutting down the program used to surf the Net.

It filters newsgroups, Web sites, IRC, FTP and e-mail by key word. It logs children's use of the Internet and can control the time spent on-line. It can also be set to monitor use of other programs.

Net Nanny did the best job of any program except SOS KidProof on protecting system settings from children's changes, and it was noticeably faster than KidProof during operation. It allows parents to remove from the computer's display parts of the Start Menu, task bar, My Computer, Windows Explorer and specific command files.

Parents can set different options for what happens when each child attempts to view a filtered site, but the lists used to filter sites are the same for all users. The program blocks the transmission of personal information.

Net Nanny 3.1; Net Nanny Software, **www.netnanny.com**, 1-800-340-7177 (11 a.m.-8 p.m. Monday-Friday); $39.95. Requires Windows 3.1/95/98, 486, 4 MB RAM, 4 MB hard disk.

SOS KIDPROOF: KidProof was the slowest of any filtering software we tested. Running every site through the KidProof server to be checked added noticeable waits to every page we visited, which could get annoying fairly quickly on a standard modem connection to the Internet.

KidProof did a nice job of preventing children from messing with system settings ranging from changing the computer's wallpaper to editing the registry. It includes total time limits and time allowed per session, as well as allowed hours of the day for surfing. It uses allow lists and block lists that you compile. Its key word lists are editable; it doesn't come with site lists. KidProof can restrict access to specific programs.

The system options can be customized for each user, but the key word lists used for blocking sexual content are the same for all users. Each person gets a single setting, based on whether the primary use is for home, office or education and whether the filtering level is high, medium or low.

If you want to see a log of sites visited, your family will need to use KidProof's own browser instead of Internet Explorer or Netscape. That browser was a bit buggy and prone to hanging in our tests. KidProof includes an easy set of instructions for restricting chat of various types.

SOS KidProof; Sterling Strategic Solutions, **www.soskidproof.com**, 1-800-427-9422 (9 a.m.-6 p.m. Monday-Friday); $29.95. Requires Windows 95/98/NT, 386, 8 MB RAM, 8 MB hard disk, Internet Explorer.

SURF WATCH 3.0: SurfWatch includes basic filtering of sexually explicit, gambling-related, violence/hate, and drugs/alcohol-related Web sites, newsgroups, IRC channels and Web chat. Parents can turn any filtering topic on or off, and can opt to block all Web-based chat and IRC.

They can also restrict their children to just sites offered by the Yahooligans! site (**www .yahooligans.com**), or to just a list that parents compile.

SurfWatch can import lists of bad words or sites, comes with its own libraries and allows parents to individually add sites to the list. Lists cannot be edited. The program did a competent job of blocking all the adult sites and not blocking innocent sites with questionable words in our tests.

SurfWatch does not include capabilities for multiple users or to limit time on-line.

Surf Watch 3.0; Spyglass Inc., **www.surfwatch.com**, 1-800-458-6600 (11 a.m.-8 p.m., Monday-Friday); $49.95. Requires Windows 95/98, 386, 4 MB RAM, 8 MB hard disk; or Apple Macintosh or PowerMac with MacOS System 7.1, 8 MB RAM, 5 MB hard disk.

WEBCHAPERONE 1.4: Web Chaperone allows you to specify settings for multiple adults and children. It divides children into three basic groups — child, preteen, teen — and four protection levels: maximum, medium, minimum and unprotected. Setup was quick and easy.

The program allows you to set a default time limit after which if no activity has taken place, it reverts to the most restrictive settings. It does not allow you to edit its lists of keywords and sites, but does allow you to add your own. It also tracks sites by ratings system.

Web Chaperone caught all our test sex sites, but also filtered the Traverse City Cherry Festival and the Victoria's Secret catalog in child-maximum mode. In adult-minimum, it still filtered the festival, but not the catalog.

The program allows you to cut off access to FTP, gopher, Web and newsgroup sites. It has a money-back satisfaction guarantee.

WebChaperone; RuleSpace Inc., **www.webchaperone.com** , 1-800-387-8373 (11:30 a.m.-8:30 p.m., Monday-Friday); $49.95. Requires Windows 95/98/NT, Pentium 90, 16 MB RAM.

X-STOP V.3.03: X-Stop includes basic filtering of Web, e-mail, chat, newsgroups and FTP sites for pornography, hate and violence. It handled our bad-site and innocent-site tests with aplomb. X-Stop filters outgoing messages for the same key words that incoming transmissions are screened with.

Parents can add or subtract specific sites or words from XStop's lists, but can't browse the lists. The data are automatically updated daily, or as often as the family goes on-line.

X-Stop was easy to install and use, but lacked the features common to more sophisticated programs, such as usage timers or the ability to have different profiles for different users. Adults will have to turn off X-Stop altogether while on-line. And some error messages were in need of being proofread — one directed surfers who thought the message was a mistake to "contact the nearest supervision."

X-Stop 3.01a; Log-On Data Corp., **www.xstop.com** , 1-888-786-7999 (10 a.m.-8 p.m. Monday-Friday); $60, including one year of daily updates. Requires Windows 95/98/NT, 8 MB RAM, 4 MB hard disk. ∎

Threats on the Net

What the Internet needs is a few more people with tin stars and white horses.

If the conviction of Richard Machado is any indication, they may be on the way.

Machado was the author of a nine-line, badly spelled, exceptionally profane e-mail message that went out to at least 59 students at his California university. In it, he promised to kill them if they didn't leave the school.

Let's assume for the moment that Machado's attorneys were right: He was distraught over the carjacking death of his brother, ashamed of flunking out of the university and not intending to do anything serious when he sent the e-mail.

None of that should matter. The bottom line is, he did something illegal, threatening specific people with bodily harm. The attitude that he should get away with it just because he sent that threat by e-mail or didn't really mean it is what has given rise to the tide of puerile garbage we all deal with on the Net.

You know what I mean.

In real life, those who steal your cash can be prosecuted. On the Internet, illegal investment schemes are slow to make the hit lists of government prosecutors.

In real life, people can be held responsible for what they say and to whom they say it. Someone who deliberately threatens you can pay for it with jail time.

On the Internet, I've witnessed hundreds of so-called flames, angry messages that threaten other Net users with everything from disembowelment to less savory fates that I'd prefer not to discuss.

And those folks with the quick keystrokes but slow brains have gotten away with it. Until now.

I'm not suggesting that we censor what people say on the Net, in messages or on Web sites.

But if we, as a society, have standards about what we think is acceptable, we need to apply those standards to every medium of communication.

If people advertise illegal schemes on the Net, they should face the same penalties they would if they had advertised on TV. If they deliberately send pornographic material to children because they think it's funny, they should face consequences.

And if they threaten to kill almost 60 people via individual e-mail messages, they should be prepared for the same kind of punishment imposed on people who make threats in person, over the phone or through the U.S. mail.

The Internet has been compared to the Wild West, and a lot of us like it that way. It is truly a global town, with no government agency deciding who has entry or what material may be offered for public consumption.

People run things the way they like, and that's a great way for the Net to be.

But even the old West had rules, lines you didn't step across and lawmen to track down the fringe elements trying to ruin the frontier for everyone.

Those folks who seek, by intimidation, fraud or abuse, to prevent people from enjoying our global Internet community are today's fringe elements.

And I, for one, am welcoming the glint of tin stars on the horizon. ∎

Solving the porn problem

Want to keep kids from seeing Internet porn?

There's a simple solution that has nothing to do with censoring what folks post on the Net or making site owners liable for minors who slip past a warning screen.

These are both the desperate acts of a governing body ignorant about the Net and faced with a seemingly impossible task: regulating a medium that was deliberately designed without central authority.

But there is one area of the Net that IS regulated, and it will be the key to effective segregation of pornography. That's the process of handing out site addresses.

So a modest proposal: Identify one type of site address — say one that ends in .sex instead of the familiar .com — as strictly for adult material.

Then require folks who want to post porn to use a .sex site.

I'm joined in this idea by the folks at Ziff-Davis Network and FamilyPC, who just wrote a piece on a similar concept. You can see their take at **www.zdnet.com/anchordesk/story /story_2330.html** .

It's not a huge burden for porn businesses: They have to buy a site name anyway, and it doesn't curtail their content in the slightest.

But what it does offer is an extremely simple way for every parent in America to block any and all sex sites from their children's computers. No longer will filtering software have to rely on bad words or lists of sites.

The ability to filter .sex addresses could be built into every new version of an Internet browser.

Addresses have always been centralized, mostly because it would be horribly confusing — not to mention taxing on the Internet's network — to have two sites with the same name. The government used to parcel out those freep.com or ameritech.net addresses, but then it handed the job over to a private company under contract.

People who want a Web site have to first buy a site name, and they can't choose one that's already in use or one of a class of site names like .gov. Adding the .sex class would require fairly simple retooling of the lists of proper addresses used by Internet computers. In fact, sets of new domain names are occasionally proposed by government and other agencies, including new commercial categories like .firm. It would be a snap to implement .sex names at the same time.

The result is positive all around: Congress looks smart for solving the Net porn problem without lawsuits or huge amounts of money. Our representatives also kill the risk of spending our tax dollars by debating a bill that will just get struck down as a violation of free speech (as the Communications Decency Act was after it attempted to censor Internet porn). Folks who post porn material on

sites other than .sex addresses would be easy to prosecute.

Legitimate porn businesses would get to do whatever it is they do with their intended audience: adults.

And parents, for the first time since the explosion of the World Wide Web, would have a fair chance of controlling what their kids get to see without cutting off their access to everything that makes the Net a cool place to be. Parents would have more control over children's exposure to porn on the Net than they would to porn in magazine racks or video rental stores.

If you agree with this solution, I hope you take the time to suggest it to your elected representatives. Now is the time to do it — before Congress gets too far along its misguided path.

It's easy, it's cheap, and it makes sense. Finding .sex could be the best thing ever to happen to parents on the Net. ∎

Other fun
Net stuff

Newsgroups

Got a quick question about that leaky faucet? Want to find out how long to boil those tomatoes you're canning? You might find the answer you're looking for in an Internet newsgroup.

We've talked before about e-mail discussion lists, where the messages that people post come directly to your mailbox. Newsgroups work in much the same way — except that the messages, instead of coming to you, are posted in central locations around the Net.

There are tens of thousands of newsgroups that address virtually every topic under the sun. When you send a message, it's automatically posted at all the sites where that newsgroup is stored on the Net. Other folks read your message and reply, and you see those replies when you go back to visit the group.

Think of it as an Internet-wide collection of bulletin boards.

You may be able to see newsgroups from within your Web browser (try typing news:// on the line where you would normally enter the Web address). But most folks who read newsgroups use special software, called a newsreader, to see them.

One of the most popular newsreaders is Forte's FreeAgent, which you can download from **www.forteinc.com** and use free. To set it up, you'll need to know the name of the computer where your Internet provider stores newsgroups. You can often find that on your provider's Web site or in your start-up materials.

Once you've set up your software to see newsgroups, you'll probably have to wait through a long download: all the newsgroup titles to which your provider offers access. They can be somewhat cryptic, making it hard to choose which groups you want to browse through without knowing in advance what you're looking for.

To get help, head to **www.deja .com** on the Web. It's a constantly updated archive of newsgroup messages that you can search by key word.

So if you're interested in fixing that leaking faucet, you could search for "faucet" or "home repair" or "home improvement," and see from the messages that popped up the groups where those topics are being discussed.

Then you can head back to your newsreader and type in the name of that group. Bingo! You'll see all the messages (called articles) that others have posted recently, and gain the right to add your own.

You don't have to subscribe to a newsgroup to post a message, which is convenient when all you have is a quick question. But that also makes newsgroups handy places for people who want to post immature messages or otherwise bait ordinary folks online.

You'll quickly discover which groups are full of off-topic postings and which are full of useful, meaty discussion. Don't bother getting into arguments with others; it's not worth your time. Instead, stick with the groups where folks seem most interested in discussing the topic at hand.

One other caveat: Bulk e-mail vendors routinely scan newsgroups for e-mail addresses for their spam lists. Create a free Web-based email account at a site such as **http://mail.yahoo.com** or **www.hotmail.com** to use with your newsgroup postings.

Enter it in the setup screen for your newsreader under e-mail address (and abbreviate your name or use a nickname, if you'd prefer to keep that private as well). That way, you'll still get the mail sent by other people in the group, but your real e-mail box won't get stuffed with junk. ■

Instant messaging

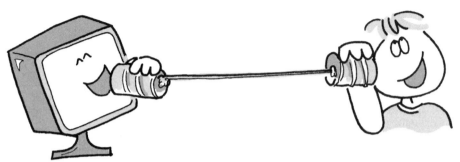

Ding! Someone's calling.

Live chat used to be synonymous with seedy chat rooms full of people talking about nothing — or about things you'd rather not think about. It brought to mind pictures of millions of America Online members with nothing to do.

Not anymore. Reborn under the more sedate title "instant messaging," private chat is making its way from teenage bedrooms to boardrooms everywhere. Families are discovering that it's a great way to keep in touch quickly, and people who work at home or on the road are discovering a way to get in on those water-cooler conversations.

Here's how it works:

You must install instant messaging software, which is free for download on the Internet. The person who wants to talk to you also has to have the same software installed — though that will soon change. New rules that will let all IM software packages talk with one another have been proposed by Microsoft and 40 other companies, but internal squabbles had delayed their release as of the publication date of this book.

Whenever you go on-line, you can choose whether you want to be available for instant messages. If you do, you tell your IM software to register you. It sends a quick message to a server computer out on the Internet. (No America Online required!)

Whenever someone hops on the Net who is interested in reaching you on-line, his or her IM program looks for your name in the registered list of people who are present.

The same goes for your software. It keeps the list of people you're seeking and constantly checks the server for their presence. A little window keeps track of your list. If someone you want to talk to hops on-line, the software changes his or her listing. To talk, you can often just double-click the person's name in your list.

When you make the call, the computer on the other end chimes to let your friend know you're there. If he or she accepts, a window pops up on both of your screens. Whatever you type in that window shows up instantly on the other person's computer.

High-end instant messaging programs (and there are more of them all the time) let you trade files or draw on a so-called virtual white board while you're chatting with someone. And some programs will allow more than two people to talk at one time.

Nearly every package lets you hide from people you don't want to talk to and lets you monitor who's tracking you on-line. Those that let you transmit files are moving toward the high-end security features you expect to see in business software, including encoding the files so they can't be intercepted during transit.

Bringing chat into the legitimate world is definitely boosting business. ICQ (say "I seek you") says that 1.4 million people use its free instant messaging software every day. It's not surprising that folks embrace the technology. It gives you the one thing that the Internet typically lacks: immediacy.

Sure, you can send people e-mail. But did they get it? And how long will you have to wait for a response? That can be vexing if you want to find out something quickly but don't want to pick up the phone. And if you want to make sure that someone positively gets that file before 5 p.m., e-mail doesn't cut it.

That's why programs like DropChute+, built by Hilgraeve in Monroe, Mich., or MediaRing Talk are taking these programs to the next level. If the person you want to talk to isn't on-line, these programs will actually call that person's computer and tell it to hop on the Net so you can exchange information automatically.

To get started in instant messaging, check out these sites for the most popular software: ICQ at **www.icq.com**, America Online (which has released a version of its IM program that doesn't require you to be a member and works over the Net) at **www.aol.com** and PeopleLink (**www.peoplelink.com**).

And the next time your computer rings, pick it up. It's for you! ▪

Get going!

It's time to get rolling on your PC. Pick an area or two where you think it could be a useful tool — balancing your checkbook, keeping you in contact with your children, researching your family tree or teaching yourself a foreign language — and get started. With a little bit of practice, you'll find that your computer can enhance your life.